cultivating
a forgiving heart

Other books in the Secrets of Soul Gardening series

Tilling the Soul: Prayer Penetrates Our Pain

Weathering the Storms: Fear Fades as Roots Deepen

secrets of soul gardening
A DEVOTIONAL STUDY

forgiveness frees us to flourish

cultivating
a forgiving heart

Denise George

GRAND RAPIDS, MICHIGAN 49530 USA

We want to hear from you. Please send your comments about this book to us in care of zreview@zondervan.com. Thank you.

ZONDERVAN™

Cultivating a Forgiving Heart
Copyright © 2004 by Denise George

Requests for information should be addressed to:
Zondervan, *Grand Rapids, Michigan 49530*

Library of Congress Cataloging-in-Publication Data

George, Denise.
    Cultivating a forgiving heart : forgiveness frees us to flourish / by Denise George.
       p. cm.—(Secrets of soul gardening)
    Includes bibliographical references (p.).
    ISBN 0-310-25117-6 (softcover)
    1. Forgiveness—Religious aspects—Christianity. I. Title.
BV4647.F55G465 2004
234'.5—dc22
                                               2004002600

Published in association with the literary agency of Alive Communications, Inc., 7680 Goddard Street, Suite 200, Colorado Springs, CO 80920.

Interior design by Beth Shagene

Printed in the United States of America

04 05 06 07 08 09 10 /❖ DC/ 10 9 8 7 6 5 4 3 2 1

For my dear friends
Pat Batson
Sandy Luster
Mary Jo Hamrick Lamberth
With appreciation for your friendship
With admiration for your unique individual gifts for ministry
And with much love

Contents

Foreword by Chuck Colson

Denise George, one of the most talented young writers I know, has tackled a subject that is at the very heart of the gospel—and at the very heart of how we live together as human beings. The gospel is the greatest story ever told because it tells us that people, weighted down with their own sin, can be forgiven at the cross and make peace with God. Many of us in America take that astounding truth for granted. It's so much a part of our culture that it is like the air we breathe. But not so in much of the world.

A number of years ago, I was in India and saw how powerful and life-transforming that message of God's forgiveness is. I was in Trivandrum in the southernmost part of the country, visiting an old British colonial era prison with huge, forbidding brick walls and iron gates. The one thousand inmates had been assembled from their grungy dormitories to sit cross-legged in the muddy field in the center of the prison. All I could see was a sea of dark skin wearing white loin cloths. Though the Indian Hindu establishment in the country does everything it can to frustrate Christian evangelism, this day I was given a royal welcome. The reason was that the superintendent of the state prison system, though a high caste Brahmin Hindu, was a great admirer of Prison Fellowship's work. He had seen lives dramatically changed in the prison. So I was escorted to the flower-bedecked platform filled with dignitaries and invited to speak to the inmates through a Hindi translator.

It was an unforgettable experience. The men stared at me wide-eyed as I talked about my own experience with Jesus and then told them how they could be forgiven of their sins, washed white as snow, and have a whole new life in Christ. Soon many of the widened eyes were filled with tears. While the Hindu officials sat solemnly on the platform, I led a thousand men in prayer to receive Christ as Savior and Lord. When I finished speaking, I wanted these men—the untouchables, outcasts in their own culture—to know that I would reach out to them. I was a former prisoner returning to greet those now incarcerated. So I jumped off the platform, startling the guards, and walked toward the men crouched on the mud field. As I reached the first man and extended my hand, all thousand men rose up like a flight of birds and completely surrounded me. For fifteen minutes, no one could get into the circle. One man would come up to me and touch me somewhere on my body, then quietly move away through the crowd as another took his place, until all one thousand men were able to make physical contact.

Why was there such a reaction? I was no celebrity. I doubt that any of those men had ever heard of Watergate. Very few of them would have known anything about President Nixon. Prison Fellowship did work in the prison, but only a small minority of men were involved. Yet most of the men had tears in their eyes as they touched me. The few who could speak English muttered something about wanting to know God.

The reason for their response had nothing to do with celebrity, but everything to do with the message. You see, in Hindu society there is no forgiveness. Hinduism teaches that what you have done wrong in this life will be done to you in the next life. It is a way in which sin and evil are perpetuated. So when a man is cast into prison, he is utterly without hope. He can never be redeemed. He will always be an outcast, and in the next life he will pay for the sins of what he has done in this life. It's the golden rule in reverse, and it is evil. It is why India is often called a Dark Continent. There is so little hope.

But this day, these men discovered the forgiveness of the gospel. The oppression that hung over that prison was lifted. That is why I say that forgiveness, grace, is the very heart of the gospel.

I've also seen how it enables people to forgive one another and be reconciled, even in the wake of the most horrendous crimes. A few years ago I was at the Carol Vance Unit in Texas, the first faith-based prison in America, initiated at the invitation of then-Governor George

Bush, with programming provided by Prison Fellowship. The program has since become a resounding success. University of Pennsylvania researchers found that the recidivism rate among those prisoners that completed the program plunged to 8 percent.

Inmates volunteer to participate in the eighteen-month course inside prison, and then they agree to work with a mentor for the first six months after their release. I was at the prison that day for the graduation of six inmates. The prison mess hall was packed with inmates, friends, visitors from the outside; one by one the graduating inmates walked forward as their names were read and I handed them their certificates. As one inmate was walking toward me, a tall, handsome woman stood and also approached me. I recognized her as Mrs. Arna Washington, a volunteer and the mother of a young girl who had been murdered fourteen years earlier. Then I realized that the man coming up for his certificate was Ron Flowers, the very man who had murdered Mrs. Washington's daughter.

Part of the in-prison Christian training program is something we call the Sycamore Tree Project. Inmates are encouraged to confess their crimes, seek God's forgiveness, and if possible reconcile with their victims. One night Ron Flowers, who had steadfastly maintained his innocence, now, as a Christian, confessed. A meeting was later arranged with Mrs. Washington, a devout believer, and the two reconciled in a flood of tears and embraces in the prison classroom.

As Ron Flowers approached and I reached out to hand him his certificate, Mrs. Washington also reached out, drew him into an embrace, then turned and faced the crowd and said, "This is the man who murdered my daughter. He is now my brother in Christ and I'm going to adopt him as my son." It was like a moment frozen in time. At first, no one moved, then some began sobbing, others gently applauding as the inmate and the mother of his victim stood before them. It was a vivid symbol of the reconciling power of Christ.

Indeed, Ron Flowers was released from prison and Mrs. Washington was good to her word. She stood up for him at his wedding. He visited her weekly. They were cemented together in a way that only Christ could achieve. And when Mrs. Washington went home to be with the Lord in 2001, Ron mourned the loss of his adopted mom.

That's why I can so enthusiastically commend this book to you. What Denise has done is take this subject so central to the gospel, and so central to how we live in the world today, and make it easily accessible for every reader. The message is put forth plainly, the illustrations are moving, and the steps for application are practical and useful. If you take the time to go through this book, which I strongly recommend you do, you will come closer to the heart of God, both in your relationship with him and in your relationship with others. You will discover the wonderful, liberating power of the gospel, the freedom that those inmates in that dingy Indian prison found, and the reconciling power that Mrs. Washington and Ron Flowers discovered in the aftermath of unthinkable tragedy.

It is a wonderful message, wonderfully told in this book.

Cultivating a Forgiving Heart

Every gardener knows that gardens must be constantly cultivated in order to produce fruits, flowers, and vegetables. A gardener must pull up uninvited weeds that grow alongside the valuable plants. Weeds come like thieves in the night. They send deep roots into the ground, choking the good plants, shadowing their sunlight, stealing their nutrients, and sometimes poisoning their soil. If allowed to grow in a garden, weeds will kill, rob, and destroy fruits and flowers. A gardener must carefully and continually tend to a garden. Careful cultivation is crucial to the life of producing plants.

A Christian's heart is like a garden. It produces fruit for Christ's kingdom. But sometimes uninvited weeds of unforgiveness spring up. They send deep roots into our soul, choking our relationship with God, shadowing the light of our witness for Christ, stealing our joy, and sometimes poisoning our spirit. If allowed to grow in our hearts, weeds of unforgiveness become branches of bitterness and roots of resentment. Wild plants must be pulled up before they can take root and grow in our soul. A believer must carefully and continually tend to the heart. Careful cultivation is crucial to the life of the fruit-producing Christian.

Sometimes people can deeply hurt us. *Cultivating a Forgiving Heart* challenges the Christian to forgive an offender. It clarifies the reasons why forgiveness is so essential to a believer's heart. It illustrates how unforgiveness can rob a person of purpose, fellowship, and joy. It debunks the many myths that keep a Christian from forgiving. Myths like forgiving means the offender didn't really hurt you; forgiving means you condone or excuse the offender's hurtful act; before forgiving an offender you must "feel" forgiving, no longer be angry, and understand why the offender hurt you.

Unforgiveness hurts the Christian believer—physically, mentally, emotionally, and spiritually. Unforgiveness breeds bitterness, and bitterness can hurt those we love. Chuck Lynch writes: "Bitterness is like a rock thrown into a placid pond; after its initial splash, it sends out concentric circles that disturb the whole pond. It starts with ourselves, expands to our spouse, then to our children, friends, and colleagues."[1]

Throughout the pages of this book, you and I will examine the true meaning of forgiveness. We will see what Scripture tells us about who to forgive, why to forgive, and how to forgive. We will meet others who have wrestled with the whole concept of forgiving someone who has intentionally thrust them in a life-threatening situation. We'll read about Christians who struggle day-to-day to forgive their offenders in an ongoing way—critical and abusive spouses, spiteful mothers-in-law, and others.

In *Cultivating a Forgiving Heart,* we will join hands and together embark upon the journey of forgiving those offenders we desperately want and need to forgive. My prayer is that this book will in some way encourage you, and that these words will give you hope and will keep you forgiving throughout life's trying times.

Acknowledgments

With much appreciation to Cindy Hays Lambert, my editor at Zondervan. Thank you, Cindy, for the sheer joy of working with you. You are an editorial genius and a good friend! A thank you also goes to Zondervan's Autumn Miller and Angela Scheff for your extensive "hands-on work" with this manuscript. Your thoughtful labor made it a much better book.

My special gratitude to Dr. and Mrs. Calvin Miller—professor, scholar, author, artist, and friend. Thanks, Calvin and Barb, for opening your beautiful home and extraordinary gardens to me while I worked on this book.

I also want to thank family and friends who prayed for this project. Your prayers and encouragement mean a lot to me.

And, as always, a special thanks to my husband, Timothy, and my lovely daughter, Alyce Elizabeth. I would also like to take this opportunity to thank my son, Christian, who graduated from Sanford University on the morning of December 13, and his new wife, Rebecca Bayne Pounds, whom he married that evening. Congratulations Christian and Rebecca! May your life together be one of fruit-bearing for the Savior.

The kingdom of heaven is like a man who sowed good seed in his field. But while everyone was sleeping, his enemy came and sowed weeds among the wheat, and went away. When the wheat sprouted and formed heads, then the weeds also appeared. The owner's servants came to him and said, "Sir, didn't you sow good seed in your field? Where then did the weeds come from?"
"An enemy did this," he replied.

A parable told by Jesus (Matthew 13:24–28)

Before You Begin

I learned to forgive in a garden. As a child, I had an argument with my younger cousin. She told me if I didn't apologize, I couldn't come to her fifth birthday party that day. I was too proud, even at age six, to say "I'm sorry." I decided instead to miss my cousin's party.

Later that afternoon, as I sat sullenly on the sofa, hearing the birthday festivities next door, my grandmother Mama (pronounced "MAW-maw") designed a teachable moment to talk with me about forgiveness. She took me to her gardens. We often talked and prayed as we walked hand-in-hand through her fragrant blooms on long summer afternoons. Mama planted healthy spiritual seeds deep into my heart's tender soil during my early years of life. Those seeds took deep root, and even now blossom with discovery and insight.

"Unforgiveness is like a weed in my garden," she told me as she knelt down to pull up a handful of wild plants. "Watch for them, 'Nisey. Pull 'em up as soon as they start to seed. Don't let them grow for one minute in your garden. Or they'll ruin your flower beds."

As she had so many times before, Mama began to compare something in her flower garden to something I needed to do in my life. Today's topic was "cultivating your garden" and "pulling up weeds."

"Pull up those weeds while they're young," Mama continued. "Get 'em before they put down roots. For once they grow roots, they're much harder to pull up. And pull 'em up completely, 'Nisey, not just by their heads, but by their long roots too. Otherwise, they'll sprout new heads and grow deeper roots."

Before the afternoon had ended, I had learned more about weeds than I ever wanted to know. With hoe in hand, Mama taught me that weeds are smart and strong and deadly, that they smother and crush and destroy everything good that grows in a garden. That they'll sneak into our flower beds and take complete control.

She also told me that weeds shoot up faster than flowers, crowding out growing space in fertile soil, sending out generations of infant off-spring—brat-babies that will play and plant themselves beside our flowers and turn our flower beds into cribs of corruption.

"Weeds are tricky," she said. "See how that lamb's-quarter weed looks like a radish? And see how that sorrel looks like spinach? Weeds can disguise themselves to look like good plants so they can grow undetected."

"Who plants the weeds, Mama?" I remember asking her.

"The enemy, honey. Satan plants the weeds." She bent down to pull up a bunch of Bermuda grass. "The enemy wants to choke out all the beauty in our gardens. He wants to fill it instead with bitter weeds."

Even at my young age, I sensed a theological lesson was coming.

"And that's just like unforgiveness, 'Nisey," she said. "The enemy wants to fill our hearts with weeds of hate and bitterness, resentment and guilt. He wants to stop our fellowship with Jesus and to break up our friendships with others. He wants to mess up our ministries, wreck our witness, and destroy our lives."

Mama pointed to the Bermuda grass. "See this?" she said. "If we leave this Bermuda grass in our garden, it'll send its poison into the ground and hurt our other plants. It's the same with this velvet leaf. It holds poison on its leaves that washes into the soil when it rains."

"'Nisey," she said, "nothing good comes from weeds—or unforgiveness. Get the weeds out of your garden, and get the unforgiveness out of your heart!"

Before evening on that memorable day, I had apologized to my cousin and wolfed down the saved piece of birthday cake.

I remembered Mama's wise words as I grew up and became an adult. Mama died when I was thirty-two, only ten days before I gave birth to my only daughter—her namesake, Alyce. During the years after her death, my husband and I lived far away from home. Going to school, getting started in careers, and birthing and rearing babies kept us far too busy to visit Mama's deserted home place. More than a decade after her death, I finally revisited my grandmother's gardens. I guess I expected them to be as beautiful and bountiful as before. But they weren't. No one had tended her flower beds. I saw firsthand how weeds can ruin a garden. Weeds, strong and thick and uninterrupted in their growth, towered over the gardens. Fruits and flowers had been choked out, smothered, and destroyed. Unguarded generations of good-for-nothing weeds had spewed out scores of shiftless offspring. Gone was everything good and lovely and valuable. The enemy had won. Bitter weeds thrived where beauty and bulbs once bloomed.

As you read the devotions and work through the Bible study sections of this book, I pray you will guard your heart from the weeds of unforgiveness. For the enemy aches to sow Bermuda grass where beauty now blossoms. Be cautious of what grows in your soul. Be aware of the enemy's tricks, for he can disguise himself and make bitterness look like helpful anger and resentment look like deserved justice. We must keep our hearts' gardens cultivated with the sharp hoe of forgiveness. Forgiveness is an action we choose to do. When we forgive people, we willingly let them off the hook for hurting us. We choose to let go of the offenses and to release the offenders from the painful debts. We purposely decide to forgive rather than to retaliate with pain. Forgiving an offender is an act of the will, and forgiveness plants the seeds of peace and freedom in our hearts. Forgiveness is a journey, a process. And the journey can sometimes be a long, difficult one.

Are you grappling with the decision to forgive someone who is currently intentionally hurting you, or has recently hurt you, or has hurt you in the distant past? Are you trying to forgive someone who purposely hurt your spouse or child or parent or friend? I know few women who have escaped the trauma of hurts, both intentional and unintentional. Hurtful offenses come in all shapes and sizes. They all need our unconditional forgiveness. Forgiveness isn't easy, but, as we will discover, it is always necessary. We forgive those who hurt us because it helps us. It frees us from the weeds of resentment and bitterness. We are the ones who benefit when we choose to forgive our offenders.

Perhaps you are wondering whether or not you should forgive someone. Perhaps you have a friend or loved one who struggles with the concept of forgiveness. Maybe you are nursing a past injury, one that has haunted you for years. You want to put it behind you and get on with your life, but you don't know how. I've found that forgiveness is usually not a one-time, isolated event, but a practice we will be called to employ repeatedly during our lifetime. Some offenses can be simply and quickly addressed, forgiven, and resolved. Others, however, can be complicated and not so easily resolved. You and I may struggle for years in our efforts to forgive. In some cases, we may need the guidance of a wise Christian friend or counselor to help us forgive and bring resolution.

In *Cultivating a Forgiving Heart,* we will discover how true forgiveness can free us so we may flourish in our faith, in our families, and in our futures. Jesus calls us to forgive, and when we choose to forgive, we are rewarded with a heart full of God's peace. Forgiveness isn't just a Christian obligation. Forgiveness is the path to personal peace and to soul serenity.

During these next six weeks, you will be invited to name your offenders and describe their various offenses to you. Then we will journey toward forgiving each offender. By the end of the book, my hope is that you will have forgiven each one.

How to Use This Book

Let's seek our answers in a sabbath of ease. Brew yourself a cup of tea. Take off your shoes. Find a chair that softly "swallows" you. Each week we will take time to bask in "daily sunlight," be sustained by a "weekly watering," and be nourished by a "weekend feeding."

Daily Sunlight

This section is for personal interaction with God, as a Bible study to work through alone or with a friend or group of friends. I pray this devotional Bible study will help you grow deeper spiritual roots. I urge you to take a few minutes to reflect on the Scriptures you encounter. You can try to answer the thought-provoking questions, or use them to stimulate discussion if you are meeting with a group.

Weekly Watering

The weekend Bible studies are to blend with your Saturday/Sunday schedule. I know you're busy, but all growing Christians, just like growing plants, need a weekly watering with the Word. God's Word is necessary to your life and mine, just as water is necessary to the life of a plant. Sometimes just a light sprinkling will do. Other times, you and I may need a good long soaking. You decide. Spend as little time or as much time as you wish on this section. Work through it by yourself, or with a friend, spouse, child, parent, or neighbor. You can also use it with a group of your friends, either in your church or community, or at a prayer retreat.

Weekend Feeding

On Sundays, a day usually graced by Bible study and church worship, there is a simple prayer. For people, as with plants, a special weekend feeding takes only a few minutes, but it provides rich nourishment all week long. In your weekend quiet time take five minutes to allow the food of this prayer to nourish your spirit, to help sustain you in your pain, and to help you grow roots more deeply in Christ.

I pray that this devotional Bible study will help you to better understand the biblical concept of forgiveness, will enable you to separate facts from myths, will empower you to choose forgiveness as a way of life, and will free you to flourish in your faith.

discovering the true
meaning of *forgiveness*

Forgiveness Is a Choice We Make

God Chooses to Forgive Us

We Must Choose to Forgive Others

The hardest thing we'll ever do

If you can forgive me then I'll know what you say is true, that God forgives me.

A former Nazi guard

World history records sadistic, cruel offenders since the beginning of civilization. One such person was a Nazi guard who wreaked havoc on Corrie ten Boom and her sister, both prisoners in a German concentration camp during World War II.

Corrie and her Christian Dutch family were arrested for offering sanctuary to the Jews in Amsterdam when Hitler rounded up Jewish people and sent them to his death camps. Nazi guards killed Corrie's mother, father, and sister. Corrie somehow survived the ordeal. And she thought she had forgiven her Nazi abusers.

After the war, Corrie received invitations to tell her concentration camp experience in churches around Europe. In her testimony, she urged her audiences to forgive those who caused them past hurts.

One Sunday night at a church service in Munich, Corrie stayed to talk to the people who had just heard her testimony. In the crowd, she recognized the former Nazi guard who had abused her. The very sight of him made her sick to her stomach, and she froze. The guard also recognized Corrie. He walked up to her, smiled, and held out his hand. Corrie kept her hands close by her side. She dared not shake his hand. Corrie trembled as he told her he had found a new faith in Jesus Christ. "Fraulein," he said and looked her in the eye, "if you can forgive me then I'll know what you say is true, that God forgives me."[1]

Corrie had to make a choice. She had just spoken on forgiveness. Yet, at that moment, she discovered she was incapable of forgiving this abusive guard who had caused her so much pain. She remembered his cruel mistreatment and wanted to turn her back to him and leave him standing in the church aisle unforgiven for his monstrous sins.

"In her mind's eye she could see her father and sister, who were both killed by the Nazis. She'd wanted to forgive what had happened to her ... [but] this moment brought insight as to why she'd been unable to do more than speak hollowly about forgiveness. She was daily reliving the horror of the camp. In that moment, too, Corrie knew that she would continue to be haunted by old feelings and memories if she did not move beyond them. This was her chance ... but could she do it?"[2]

Her arm remained frozen at her side. But Corrie knew that God had forgiven her. She also knew that, as a Christian, she must forgive this man. It would be the hardest thing she ever had to do. Corrie bowed her head and said a silent prayer. She begged God to give her the grace to forgive this former Nazi, the same grace God had extended toward her.

After her prayer, Corrie felt a new sense of strength in her heart, a fresh desire to forgive this offender who had once so brutally beaten her. She looked him in the face, reached out and clasped his hand, and gave him the gift of forgiveness.

"In that moment," she later wrote, "something miraculous happened. A current seemed to pass from me to him, while into my heart sprang a love for this stranger that almost overwhelmed me."[3]

Corrie no longer saw this man with human eyes. She suddenly saw him with God's eyes. Yes, he had wounded her. He had caused her and her family unbelievable pain. But God had forgiven him and brought him into his family. He was now her brother in Christ. Love filled Corrie's heart for her newfound forgiven brother. From that day forward, her testimony—her words about forgiveness—took on new energy and new meaning.

After the war years, Corrie took care of other victims of Nazi cruelty. She loved them, cared for them in her own home, and urged them to forgive their cruel captors. She made a remarkable discovery about the benefits of forgiveness. She saw that "those who were able to forgive their former enemies were able also to return to the outside world and rebuild their lives, no matter what the physical scars. Those who nursed their bitterness remained invalids. It was as simple and as horrible as that."[4]

You need not spend time in a German Nazi concentration camp in order to understand the massive hurt other people can cause you. You may be suffering right now. Hurts are real and deep and significant whether they include imprisonment and physical torture, or a husband's or child's lie or betrayal. During the next six weeks, we will work through the process of forgiveness. We will see how forgiveness will free you from weeds of bitterness and resentment.

The Bible teaches us to forgive people, like the Nazi guard, who have purposely caused unnatural or shocking cruelty to us. God's Word also teaches us to forgive people like unappreciative children or selfish husbands or hateful coworkers, who dish out day-to-day abuses. Only with God's help can you and I forgive those who wound us or hurt those we love.

Do you know someone you need to forgive? Has a parent, spouse, child, sibling, neighbor, employer, employee, church member, or stranger hurt you? We all have enemies. As you have, no doubt, already discovered, we can't live long in this world without the need to forgive an offender.

Daily Sunlight

@ Interact with the Gardener

Read what Paul writes in Romans 12:14. Ask God to bring to mind anyone in your life whose hurtful actions linger unforgiven in your heart. On index cards, write the names of the people in your life who are currently persecuting or, in some way, mistreating you. Use one card per person. Beneath each name write the mistreatment inflicted on you by that person. Take your time. Do not hesitate to add a card even if that event is in your distant past. You will use these cards over the next few weeks on your journey to forgiveness.

@ Time to Grow

List all the reasons why Corrie ten Boom could have chosen not to forgive the Nazi guard.

In what ways did Corrie follow Paul's advice when she decided to forgive the guard?

In what ways does Corrie's remarkable forgiveness of the persecuting guard help you with your struggle to forgive someone who has hurt you?

What did Corrie observe about those Holocaust victims who could not forgive? How does Corrie's discovery affect your own thinking about whether or not to forgive your offender?

You can learn more about Corrie's remarkable ministry and journey of forgiveness in her book, *The Hiding Place*.

@ Prayer

Jesus, I have before me the names of all those people who are hurting me or in some way mistreating me. I want to choose to forgive them, Lord. I want the freedom from bitterness that your Word promises me. But how hard it is to "bless those who persecute" me! How is it possible, Lord? I am willing to try, Father. Please walk with me through this journey. In Jesus' name, amen.

Forgiveness is a journey

Forgiving is a journey, sometimes a long one, and we may need some time before we get to the station of complete healing, but the nice thing is that we are being healed en route. When we genuinely forgive, we set a prisoner free and then discover that the prisoner we set free was us.

Lewis B. Smedes

Twenty-two-year-old Jennifer deeply loved her fiancé, Troy. He was a kind and loving Christian man, a hard worker, and her best friend. She spent almost a year planning their wedding. Standing at the church altar, looking into his eyes, and vowing to love him forever, Jennifer thought their life together would be perfect. Everything went smoothly—until the honeymoon ended. That's when Troy's mother, Maureen, started to interfere in the newlyweds' happy lives.

Maureen became her daughter-in-law's worst nightmare. She stopped by their apartment without calling first. She invited herself to dinner and then criticized Jennifer's cooking skills. Jennifer tried to be loving and caring. She tried to follow the apostle Paul's teachings when he advised, "Be kind and compassionate to one another" (Eph. 4:32). But Maureen became too much for Jennifer to handle.

Out of courtesy, and because Troy had requested it, Jennifer invited Maureen to the first dinner party she arranged for their friends. Jennifer spent a week cleaning the apartment, polishing her new pieces of wedding-gift silver, shopping for steak and fresh vegetables, and baking a special chocolate fudge cake. Jennifer put the food on the table and gracefully seated their guests. The dinner party got off to a good start.

And then Maureen started to talk. She talked and talked, interrupting anyone else who tried to say a word. For more than an hour, Maureen hardly took a breath. She didn't give anyone else a chance to speak. She even made some cutting remarks to Jennifer in front of her friends.

"Jen," she asked, "what did you marinate your steak in, dear? It seems a little tough."

"Jen," she asked, "are these veggies fresh or were they frozen? They seem a little limp. How long did you cook them?"

Maureen criticized the food throughout the meal. When Jennifer, almost on the verge of tears, served her special cake, Maureen said she didn't want any. "Sugar is just so bad for the human body," she told Jennifer. "That cake looks like it's loaded with sugar."

Later that night in their bedroom, Jennifer broke down and cried. "Troy, your mother ruined our dinner party. Did you hear how she criticized me all through the dinner?"

"Oh Jen," Troy said. "She didn't mean anything by it. You're just too sensitive."

For the following five years, Maureen spent a lot of time with the young couple. She continued to criticize Jennifer. When Jennifer took a good-paying job to help out with expenses, Maureen told her she should stay home and take better care of her house and husband. When Jennifer decided to leave her job and stay home, Maureen criticized her for not helping Troy with the expenses. Jennifer couldn't seem to win.

Day after day Jennifer tried to be kind and compassionate to Maureen. But inside, Jennifer wanted to explode. She hated the way her mother-in-law criticized her. She grew angry at the way Troy defended his mother, especially when he told Jennifer not to be so sensitive.

But the real problems started when Jennifer gave birth to their first child. Maureen moved into their apartment for a while to help them out. Maureen took over caring for the baby. If Jennifer put a blanket on the newborn, Maureen said the baby was too hot. When Jennifer took the blanket off the baby, Maureen told her the child was too cold. Even after Maureen moved back out, Jennifer's stomach stayed tied in knots whenever she encountered her critical mother-in-law.

Do you have someone in your life who criticizes you and keeps your stomach in knots? An in-law or parent or child or spouse? Is this person someone you must put up with on a day-to-day basis? If so, you can understand just how Jennifer felt—frustrated, angry, and bitter.

Jennifer finally scheduled an appointment to talk with her Bible study leader, Margaret, a biblically wise woman. She explained the situation. She admitted she didn't know what to do, or how to deal with her mother-in-law. Margaret gave her some good advice.

"You are right, Jennifer, to be kind and compassionate to your mother-in-law. She's your husband's mother and your son's grandmother. As long as she lives, she will always be a part of your life. But I think you need to do two things. One is to work closely with Troy to establish some healthy boundaries for Maureen's access to your daily lives. But more important, you need to forgive her."

"I should forgive her?!" Jennifer blurted out. "What does forgiveness have to do with the way she treats me?"

"As long as you hold on to your resentment toward her, you will be the prisoner in your own home. When you decide to forgive her, you'll be the one who is set free. You may not be able to change her, but you'll see a big difference in the way you feel toward her," Margaret explained.

Jennifer took Margaret's advice. She and Troy decided to set some stricter privacy boundaries in their life. Together, in consultation with Margaret, they offered Maureen less access over their personal lives. They set new limits and worked together to enforce them.

It wasn't easy to forgive Maureen. It was a day-to-day process. But every time Maureen criticized her, Jennifer whispered a prayer. "Lord, I forgive Maureen for making that mean critical statement. I choose not to allow her to make my life miserable. I choose not to resent her. I choose not to hold a grudge. Help me, Lord, not to take her criticism personally. Help me to deal with her verbal jabs." Maureen continued to find fault with just about everything Jennifer did. But Jennifer found herself changing her feelings toward Maureen. Slowly, she came to see her critical mother-in-law with Jesus' eyes. She began to feel sorry for her. She looked more deeply into Maureen's life and discovered Maureen had no friends. Maureen was lonely.

Jennifer dedicated herself to praying more often for Maureen. She asked God to bless Maureen. Years passed by as Jennifer prayed for Maureen. Her mother-in-law never changed. She actually became harsher, more self-centered, and more judgmental. But Jennifer changed. She kept forgiving and praying for Maureen, over and over again, until she had pulled up those weeds of bitterness that had grown deep into her heart. One day, Jennifer actually caught herself smiling when Maureen criticized the tough steak, overcooked vegetables, and sugary dessert. Jennifer had found freedom through her decision to forgive. It was a long journey, but Jennifer found healing. It was worth the effort.

Is there someone in your own life that you need to forgive and pray for? A hateful coworker, a nosy neighbor, a gossipy church member, a spiteful sister-in-law? Your forgiveness and prayers might not change your offender's behavior, but it will definitely change your own heart.

Daily Sunlight

@ Interact with the Gardener

Do you currently have someone in your life like Jennifer's mother-in-law, Maureen? Someone who criticizes you, belittles you in front of others, and generally makes your day-to-day life miserable? Did you make an index card for that person yesterday? If not, do so now. List the person's characteristics that hurt or irritate you.

@ Time to Grow

Think about the person you described as you read the apostle Paul's advice in Ephesians 4:31–32: "Get rid of all bitterness, rage and anger, brawling and slander, along with every form of malice. Be kind and compassionate to one another, forgiving each other, just as in Christ God forgave you." Read it in several different translations. Name some of the ways the psalmists (throughout the book of Psalms), describe their cruel offenders. (Read at least four of the following Scriptures and record your initial reactions.)

- Psalm 1:4–6
- Psalm 3:1, 7

- Psalm 5:4–6, 9–10
- Psalm 6:8–10
- Psalm 9:13–18
- Psalm 10:1–11
- Psalm 17:8–14
- Psalm 18:47–49
- Psalm 22:6–7

Throughout these psalms, what do the psalmists ask God to do to their offenders?

How does God comfort the offended in their distress?

Pen your own psalm to God. Be as frank with the Lord as the psalmists are. Describe to him your enemies and your offenders. Pray for God's protection and wisdom in forgiving them.

℮ Prayer

Father, I feel bitterness in my heart whenever I think of [name your offender]. Show me how to extend kindness and compassion. Show me how to take the apostle Paul's advice and get rid of the rage and anger I feel for this person. I want to be free from the prison of bitterness. But I don't know how. I don't know where to start. Show me how, Lord, for I am willing to try. In Jesus' name, amen.

Three essential elements

> Forgiveness is "the act of setting someone free from an obligation to you that is a result of a wrong done against you." ... [It] involves three elements: injury, a debt resulting from the injury, and a cancellation of the debt. All three elements are essential if forgiveness is to take place.
>
> Charles Stanley

What happens when we decide not to forgive? We encounter the three ugliest words in the English language: *revenge, reprisal,* and *retaliation.*

Revenge and reprisal seek to injure the person who has injured us. When we seek revenge or reprisal, we become avengers who inflict injury.

Retaliation seeks to return evil for evil—blow for blow, insult for insult, harm for harm. If you knock out my eye, I will knock out your eye. If you break my tooth, I will break your tooth. That's retaliation.

Revenge, reprisal, and retaliation often start ridiculous murderous feuds. They pile pain upon pain, all in the name of payback revenge.

Wyatt Earp and Billy Clanton started a deadly feud when Earp caught Clanton riding his stolen horse. It ended in a shoot-out at Tombstone's O.K. Corral in October 1881. Clanton was killed. Earp became famous.

The Hatfields and McCoys aren't sure why they started their feud back in the 1800s on the Kentucky–West Virginia border. Some say the two Appalachian families fought over a stolen pig. The two families hated each other. Revenge, reprisal, and retaliation became their vocations, their accepted lifestyles.

During the Civil War, West Virginia's Hatfields fought with the Confederates. Kentucky's McCoys fought with the Union. In 1875, Harmon McCoy was killed. Although no one knew who killed him, his death further fueled the feud. For more than a century after McCoy's death, the families hated and fought each other, avenged and killed each other. The children of the Hatfields and McCoys continued the battle long after the original feuders died. The final confrontation between the families came in 2000! They disputed over access to a cemetery. They battled it out in court.

Not until June 14, 2003, did the feud finally end. Representatives of both families came together and signed a truce. Reo Hatfield and Bo McCoy drafted a treaty that proclaimed: "[We] do hereby and formally declare an official end of all hostilities, implied, inferred and real, between the families, now and forevermore."

On that day, West Virginia's governor, Bob Wise, and Kentucky's governor, Paul Patton, proclaimed June 14, 2003, as Hatfield–McCoy Reconciliation Day.[5]

Being lured and baited into aggression and revenge is the loss of real power. The momentary feeling of satisfaction that you may feel in an act of reprisal is counterfeit and short-lived, and the end result is that you—the retaliator—become the victimizer, the very thing you abhorred at the start. As John Claypool writes, "Our first instinct when we are badly hurt by another is to want to do the same in return, but when we are seduced into imitating what we abhor, we only increase the amount of damage that was there in the first place."[6]

Does avenging feel better than forgiving? Perhaps for some, avenging feels better in the immediate emotional release of satisfaction since the distasteful emotion of being the victim sometimes falsely masquerades as the feeling of weakness. Retaliation is the act of becoming the aggressor. It gives a false sense of power and control. But that feeling is a lie. True power exists in self-control.

Know that the Lord helps you to forgive. He helps you to be merciful, to pardon, to forgive the ones who deserve the harshest punishment. He helps you to forgive your friends who betray your confidence, your fellow church members who whisper secrets about you behind your back, your neighbors who leave you out of their social circles, your employer who makes your nine-to-five workdays miserable.

When you forgive people who hurt you, you give them a gift they do not deserve. Three essential elements must happen when you choose to forgive.

First, you must be injured. You need to acknowledge to yourself that you have been injured. Not by mistake or accident, but by an offender's deliberate choice. We *excuse* accidents and mistakes. But we *forgive* the purposeful pain caused by another human being.

Second, you must acknowledge to yourself that the offender owes you a debt. The person has *purposely* hurt you.

Third, forgiving the offender means you *cancel the debt*. You *release* the person from the payment. You give the miracle of *pardon* and set the offender free from the owed debt. Mercy given, grace granted—it's a mysterious process, one that goes against our human instincts. The person certainly doesn't deserve your forgiveness, but you give your forgiveness anyway.

Acknowledging you have been injured and that the offender owes you a debt, forgiving the offender and canceling the debt—these actions bring about complete forgiveness. And complete forgiveness—no matter how long the process takes—brings you an indescribable freedom.

We are to choose to forgive someone who has hurt us:

1. God, in Christ, has forgiven you (Eph. 4:32).
2. Christ asks you to forgive others (Luke 6:36).

You give the gifts of mercy, love, and generosity even though the wrongdoer deserves to be punished. Rather than demanding an "eye for an eye," a "tooth for a tooth," you overcome the evil act with goodness and forgiveness. Normal human response is revenge and we desire to retaliate with pain. A debt is owed, whether or not the offender acknowledges it, admits it, or confesses it. Have you ever wanted to get even with someone who has hurt you? If so, you're not alone. Revenge is an automatic human reflexive urge.

Grace Ketterman and David Hazard explain it as a *talionic* impulse. "The term comes from a root word that means 'to punish in a way that exacts a penalty corresponding in kind to the crime . . . as in the principle of an eye for an eye.' From this root we also get the word *retaliate,* which refers to our innate impulse to strike back, to make someone else repay with an 'eye for an eye, a tooth for a tooth'—and, frankly, even more if we can get it."[7]

Revenge is as old as civilization itself. Adam and Eve's son Cain hated and resented his brother Abel. Cain saw that God accepted Abel's lamb offerings and refused his own fruit offerings. He was jealous. He wanted to retaliate. He wanted revenge.

"Why are you angry?" the Lord asked Cain. "Why is your face downcast?" (Gen. 4:6). Cain's need for revenge resulted in his killing his brother Abel (Gen. 4:8).

In Old Testament days, to protect the accused, Moses made certain laws regarding personal injury. Take an "eye for eye, tooth for tooth, hand for hand, foot for foot, burn for burn, wound for wound, bruise for bruise," he told Israel's people (Exod. 21:24–25). Otherwise, revenge might take a life for an eye; a life for a tooth; a life for a hand, foot, burn, wound, or bruise. While the law sounds like permission to avenge an offender, the law actually put strict limits on revenge. It protected the offender from death after he injured another person.

Jesus taught us a new way to live, a way free from hurt, retaliation, and revenge. He asked us to love others and to forgive those who hurt us.

"You have heard that it was said, 'Eye for eye, and tooth for tooth,'" he said. "But I tell you, Do not resist an evil person. If someone strikes you on the right cheek, turn to him the other also" (Matt. 5:38–39).

Nothing good comes from revenge. Revenge only feeds feuds and fuels further retaliation. We must not repay evil with more evil, hate with more hate. Forgiveness, on the other hand, loves and disarms the offender. It stops the ache for reprisal.

Hatred leads to reprisal and violence. Reprisal and violence lead to even more hatred. The circle of hate can go on for years, centuries, even millennia. It's the way of the world.

The unnatural act of forgiveness, however, is the way of Christ.

Daily Sunlight

℮ Interact with the Gardener

Consider the people you listed on index cards on Monday and Tuesday. According to Charles Stanley, forgiveness involves three elements: *injury,* a *debt* resulting from the injury, and a *cancellation* of the debt. Review your cards. On each card you listed the name of the offender and the mistreatment that offender caused you. Now write on each card the debt that person owes you.

Read Hebrews 10:30–31. What does this passage say to you? Who is the one responsible for avenging evildoers? Who is the only one who deserves the right to avenge?

℮ Time to Grow

Alistair Begg, in *The Hand of God,* writes: "If we are harboring unforgiveness toward someone, we'll find that our usefulness in the kingdom of God is sadly diminished."[8] In what ways has your own unforgiving heart interrupted your usefulness in God's kingdom?

How does an unforgiving heart affect your relationship with God?

Does your Christian witness or testimony suffer because of unforgiveness? How?

Before you can enter into the process of forgiving your persecutors, you must clearly understand the injury they caused you, as well as the debt they now owe you. Once you have clearly identified the injury and debt, you can begin the forgiveness process.

Reflect for a moment on your offenders. Think about what punishment each one deserves. How would you want to retaliate if you allowed your old human nature to take charge? Write your response on the cards by each offender's name.

@ **Prayer**

Father, my old human nature wants to lash out at my persecutors. I want revenge and reprisal. Lord, help me to fight against the sinful nature that wants to get even with those who hurt me. I am your daughter, and as your daughter you call me to deal with my offenders in a Christlike way. Show me, Lord, how to accomplish this goal. In Jesus' name, amen.

A man called Stephen

I have been crucified with Christ and I no longer live, but Christ lives in me. The life I live in the body, I live by faith in the Son of God, who loved me and gave himself for me.

Galatians 2:20

What is your definition of forgiveness? I like to explain forgiveness with this example: Take a piece of chalk and scribble on a clean blackboard. Think of your messy scribbling as a friend's hurtful actions toward you—a lie to your face, a slanderous statement behind your back, a betrayal of trust—ugly offenses you didn't deserve. When you make the decision to forgive the one who hurt you, you take a wet rag and completely wash all the scribbles off the blackboard. You wash the slate clean, erasing that lie or slander or betrayal, and putting the offender's wrongful actions behind you. That's forgiveness. Washing the blackboard doesn't mean you are pretending the offense didn't happen. It did, and it hurt you deeply. But you are choosing to release the offender from the offense, the debt owed to you.

Forgiving someone may not happen overnight, especially when the crime against you is great. But *choosing* to forgive takes only a second. When you make that life-changing choice, the process of forgiveness begins. When you make the decision to forgive, you embark on a mysterious journey.

What makes this journey of forgiveness a mystery? Forgiving a hate-filled, cruel offender baffles our sense of logic and justice. At a strictly human level, forgiveness doesn't make much sense. As we discussed yesterday, our natural instinct is to fight, avenge, and hate.

"The acts of the sinful nature are obvious," states Paul. They are "sexual immorality, impurity and debauchery; idolatry and witchcraft; hatred, discord, jealousy, fits of rage, selfish ambition, dissensions, factions and envy; drunkenness, orgies, and the like" (Gal. 5:19–21).

But when Christ came into our lives and filled up our hearts, he gave you and me a new nature. Do you remember what Paul wrote to the Christians in Corinth? "Therefore, if anyone is in Christ, there is a new creation; the old has gone, the new has come! All this is from God, who reconciled us to himself through Christ and gave us the ministry of reconciliation: that God was reconciling the world to himself in Christ, not counting people's sins against them. And he has committed to us the message of reconciliation" (2 Cor. 5:17–19 TNIV).

Our new Christ-nature has replaced our old sin-nature. Our new nature seeks the Spirit's fruit brought to us by forgiveness: love, joy, peace, patience, kindness, goodness, faithfulness, gentleness, and self-control (see Gal. 5:22–23).

Paul tells us "those who belong to Christ Jesus have crucified the sinful nature with its passions and desires" (Gal. 5:24). He urges Christians to "live by the Spirit . . . keep in step with the Spirit" (Gal. 5:25).

God's Spirit gives us the power to forgive those people that criticize us, irritate us, belittle us, deceive us, abuse us, betray us, and even seek to kill us.

Stephen was such a forgiver. Scripture describes Stephen as "a man full of God's grace and power" (Acts 6:8).

One day while Stephen preached and ministered to a crowd of people, an argument broke out between the city's leaders. They lied about Stephen to the crowd. Then they persuaded the crowd to confirm their lies. They accused Stephen of speaking words of blasphemy against God and Moses. To provoke savage violence against Stephen, they stirred up the people, the elders, and the teachers of the law. In a rage, the crowd, who thought they followed a scriptural mandate to stone a blasphemer, seized Stephen. They sentenced him to death by stoning. They rushed at him, dragged him out of the city, and pulverized him with rocks.

As Stephen lay dying, his accusers assaulted him with sharp jagged stones. Broken, bleeding, and barely conscious, he "looked up to heaven" and saw "Jesus standing at the right hand of God" (Acts 7:). Then, above the racket of the ravaging riot, Stephen prayed aloud: "Lord, do not hold this sin against them" (Acts 7:60).

Even as they tortured him to death, Stephen chose to forgive them. He decided to pardon them, to release them from the debt of their horrible crimes against him. You see, Stephen had long before been crucified with Christ. As a new creature in Christ, he willingly chose to forgive the townspeople.

Stephen's dying words of forgiveness for his killers closely resembled Jesus' own dying words. As soldiers drove spikes into his wrists, fastened him to a wooden cross, and prepared him to die a cruel death, he spoke words of forgiveness. "Father," Jesus prayed, "forgive them, for they do not know what they are doing" (Luke 23:34). Jesus forgave the offenders that caused his excruciating death.

Has someone in your life hurt you so cruelly, so brutally, so horribly that you think that person is beyond your forgiveness? The crime against you may have been so heinous you don't know how to forgive. Maybe you don't even want to forgive.

Whenever I think of a heinous brutal crime, I think of Timothy McVeigh. His horrible act brought newspaper headlines and sympathy from across the world. On April 19, 1995, McVeigh pulled up to the Oklahoma City's Alfred P. Murrah Federal Building in a rented Ryder truck loaded with fifty-five-gallon drums of ammonium nitrate. At 9 a.m., just as the new workday started and the building buzzed with people, McVeigh lit the fuse and walked away. Without emotion, he climbed into his 1977 Mercury Marquis and drove off.

Some eighty minutes later, a police officer stopped McVeigh for not having a rear license plate. Police traced the rental truck to McVeigh and arrested him.

Years after the Oklahoma City bombing, Timothy McVeigh's words and actions indicated that he felt no guilt or pain for killing 168 people, including 19 children. He even referred to the murdered children as "collateral damage." After his arrest, reporters described his face "as blank as a mannequin." When someone in the crowd screamed out "baby killer," McVeigh didn't even flinch. He remained stone-faced, defiant, and smug during his trial, sentencing, and execution by lethal injection.

He thought of himself as a hero. He refused to apologize for his premeditated mass murder.[9]

McVeigh remained unrepentant as he awaited execution on death row at the U.S. Penitentiary in Terre Haute, Indiana. His prison mate, a convicted murderer, and a new Christian, David Hammer, begged McVeigh to repent, to express regret. He urged him to seek spiritual redemption, God's forgiveness. But McVeigh refused.

"I know that David has tried his best to influence McVeigh to admit at least the fact that his acts have hurt so many people irrevocably," claimed Sister Camille D'Arienzo, who had known Hammer since 1998. "But David knows that forgiveness, even by God, seems to require some admission of guilt and plea for forgiveness."[10]

I visited the bomb site in Oklahoma City on the third anniversary of the bombing, and it broke my heart. I read the notes, touched the teddy bears, and looked at the photos pressed into the chain-link fence that surrounds the site. I have often wondered if God could ever forgive Timothy McVeigh for what he did. My friend Chuck Colson answered this question when he wrote: "To suggest that Christ's sacrifice wouldn't apply to someone like Timothy McVeigh would be to say that it doesn't apply to anyone." But, he adds: "What's missing was the sense of horror about his actions and the suffering he inflicted. It's this horror that leads one to embrace grace and seek forgiveness; without it the unrepentant remain unredeemed."[11]

I have also wondered if McVeigh ever had a change of heart. Did he repent? Did he feel anything even slightly resembling human guilt, pain, or remorse for his heinous crime? As far as we know, he died an unfeeling young man with a cold, unforgiven heart.

When you choose to forgive an unrepentant offender, you forgive the offender for your own good. You are the one who will benefit from one-sided forgiveness. Your choice to forgive, or not to forgive, will not affect the offender's feelings in any way. You and I can't make anyone feel our pain or experience guilt for a deliberate action against us. You can, in no way, make your offender suffer like you are suffering.

How hard it is to forgive a man like Timothy McVeigh! But forgiveness is always necessary, even when the crime is heinous and brutal.

Daily Sunlight

@ Interact with the Gardener

In Galatians 2:20, Paul writes about his own "crucifixion" with Christ. Write in your own words what Paul might mean by this statement.

Write down how your own "crucifixion" with Christ has changed the way you think about revenge and retaliation.

Read God's promise to us in 1 John 1:9: "If we confess our sins, he is faithful and just and will forgive us our sins and purify us from all unrighteousness." Pretend you are talking with Timothy McVeigh. Explain aloud to him what this verse means.

If Timothy McVeigh asked God for forgiveness for his crime, do you think God would have forgiven him? Why?

Can you name any offense that God refuses to forgive?

@ Time to Grow

The following Scriptures are intended to guide you into a time of reflection. Read each suggested Scripture passage and write down your immediate thoughts:

- 2 Corinthians 5:17–19: How does a person become a "new creation"? Describe the moment you decided to give your life to Christ and you became a new creation.
- Galatians 5:22–23: Make a list of the gifts the Spirit has given you when you became a new creature.
- Galatians 5:24: Describe your old human "sinful nature."

List some of the ways that you, as a new creature, have changed.

☺ **Prayer**

Father, I have been crucified with you, and you have forgiven my old sinful nature. You have made me a new creation. I pray, Father, that you will show me how to "live by your Spirit" and how to "keep in step with your Spirit." You have given me a new nature. You have endowed me with wonderful gifts of your Spirit. Help me, Lord, to be as forgiving as your child Stephen. Place my feet on the path of forgiveness and help me to show kindness and compassion to those who persecute me, even those brutal offenders like Timothy McVeigh. I will depend on your guidance, Lord. In Jesus' name, amen.

Forgiving a terrorist

Forgive us our debts, as we also have forgiven our debtors.

Matthew 6:12

Do you remember what happened to Todd Beamer on September 11, 2001? Todd and the other passengers boarded United Flight 93, expecting an uneventful flight from Newark, New Jersey, to San Francisco, California. After the crew closed the plane's door, everyone settled into seats, buckled seat belts, and prepared to take off. Todd had a business meeting in San Francisco. He sat in row ten and pecked away at his laptop while the plane sat on the runway and waited its turn. Due to heavy traffic, the plane stayed on the runway much longer than usual.

Earlier that morning, three other planes took off and headed for California. American Flight 11 and United Flight 175 left from Boston's Logan Airport at 8:00 a.m. American Flight 77 took off from Washington D.C.'s Dulles Airport at 8:10 a.m. Finally, at 8:42 a.m., air-traffic controllers gave Todd's plane permission to leave Newark.

As Todd's plane ascended over the New York–New Jersey coastline, American Flight 11 crashed into the World Trade Center's north tower. Minutes later, United Flight 175 flew straight into the World Trade Center's south tower. Terrified people screamed and cried as they ran from collapsing towers and billowing smoke. A few minutes later, American Flight 77 smashed into the Pentagon in Washington D.C. Live television news cameras covered the tragic crashes as they killed passengers in the planes and people on the ground.

All went well with United Flight 93 until knife-carrying terrorists stormed the cockpit, sliced the throats of the two pilots, and took control of the plane. Suicidal Muslim terrorists had boarded all four planes. They had a sinister, well-orchestrated plan to hijack, crash, kill, and destroy. Still airborne, terrorists herded horrified passengers on United Flight 93 to the back of the plane. The plane dipped and turned sharply off course. Passengers huddled together with their cell phones. Through their phone calls, coworkers, family members, and friends on the ground reported to United Flight 93's passengers the breaking news about the hijacked and crashed planes. Everyone thought this plane would probably follow the same pattern.

Passengers with cell phones called loved ones and said a final "I love you." Then they plotted to foil the terrorists' intentions. Even if it cost them their lives, they wouldn't allow the terrorists aboard their plane to reach its target.

As Todd Beamer's plane, only fifteen to twenty minutes from the nation's capital, careened erratically through the skies, Todd made one last phone call. He decided not to call his pregnant wife at home for fear it would upset her. Instead he phoned GTE Airfone Customer Care Center in Oakbrook, Illinois.

Todd told GTE supervisor, Lisa Jefferson, that his plane had been hijacked. While the plane plunged from its authorized altitude, tossing passengers around the cabin, Todd supplied Mrs. Jefferson with precise details. He also told her about their plan to attack the terrorists.

"In case I don't make it through this," Todd told Mrs. Jefferson, "would you please call my family and let them know how much I love them?"[12] She promised she would.

In spite of the confusion, Todd kept his Airfone connection with Mrs. Jefferson and updated her on everything that happened. Todd asked Mrs. Jefferson a question: "Would you pray with me?" She agreed. Together, from start to finish, these two strangers, one high above the earth facing his own death, and one safely on the ground listening to the horrible details, prayed in unison the Lord's Prayer.

"Our Father in heaven," they prayed over the phone, "hallowed be your name. Your kingdom come, your will be done on earth as it is in heaven. Give us today our daily bread. Forgive . . ."

Todd's next words probably shook his very soul.

"Forgive . . ."

How could he voice them? How could he pray for forgiveness for the very terrorists who planned his death?

"Forgive us our debts," he prayed, "as we also have forgiven our debtors. And lead us not into temptation, but deliver us from the evil one. Amen" (see Matt. 6:9–13).

When they finished praying, Mrs. Jefferson later reported that Todd said: "Jesus, help me."[13]

After that, Mrs. Jefferson remembers that Todd, with a sigh in his voice, took a deep breath, and called out: "Are you ready? Okay. Let's roll!"

The passengers charged the terrorists in the cockpit. The plane rocked from side to side, then flipped over. Out of control and diving sharply downward, United Flight 93 hit the ground so hard it blasted a hole in the earth fifty feet deep.

No one on the ground was killed. No buildings were destroyed. Thanks to the courageous and caring passengers aboard United Flight 93, the plane "had not crashed into the Capitol; nor had it smashed into the White House, Camp David, or any other national landmark. Instead, it crashed in an open field" in Shanksville, Pennsylvania, an abandoned coal strip mine.[14] The plane totally disintegrated. Rescue workers found few remaining plane pieces or human fragments.

That day the terrorists not only killed Todd Beamer and all the passengers aboard the plane, but they killed dreams and families and futures. Lisa Beamer lost a husband. Her two little boys and her unborn daughter lost a father. The terrorists hurt far more people than just Todd Beamer and the other passengers aboard that plane.

When Lisa Beamer learned of Todd's final prayer, she said that Todd had known the Lord's Prayer since his childhood. "Part of the prayer that intrigued Todd," she said, "was the line in which Jesus taught us to ask God to forgive our trespasses, or sins, as we forgive those who trespass against us. When Lisa [Jefferson] told me Todd had prayed that particular prayer, I felt certain that, in some way, Todd was forgiving the terrorists for what they were doing."[15]

What is forgiveness? It's plunging to the ground on a terrorist-piloted plane and forgiving ahead of time those who will be responsible for your death. "And forgive us our debts," Todd prayed, "as we also have forgiven our debtors."

Daily Sunlight

℮ Interact with the Gardener

You may never be called on to forgive a terrorist who orchestrates your death, but today I want you to think about the hurtful people you listed on index cards during Monday's Bible study. As you ponder each one, turn in your Bible to Matthew 6:9–13. Pray this personal prayer and list all the people you want to forgive.

> [My] Father in heaven,
> hallowed be your name,
> your kingdom come,
> your will be done
> on earth as it is in heaven.
> Give [me] today [my] daily bread.
> Forgive [me my] debts,
> As [I will also seek to forgive my] debtors.
> And lead [me] not into temptation,
> But deliver [me] from the evil one.

℮ Time to Grow

Reflecting on the people you just listed above, make a decision to commit to the following four suggestions:

1. Say each offender's name aloud, and pray for each one individually. (Your prayer might be something like this: "Lord, I pray for [name your offender]. You alone know this person's hurts and needs. Forgive this person, Father, for the pain this offender has brought me. Bless this person in the ways you choose. Amen.")

2. Make the decision through prayer to start the forgiveness process. (Your prayer might be something like this: "Lord, [name your

offender] has deeply hurt me. I know it will take some time for me to forgive. But I pray, Father, that you will set my feet upon the path of forgiveness, so that, one day in the future, I can completely forgive [name your offender].")

3. Review often your stack of index cards. Keep them in your Bible. During your Bible study times next week, pray each day for each offender the two prayers above.

4. Commit your heart to seek to forgive each offender on each index card.

❧ Prayer

Father, I want to rid my heart of these weeds of unforgiveness, anger, hatred, and resentment toward my offenders. I commit myself to the goal of seeking to forgive each offender. I understand that this is just the first step in my journey toward complete forgiveness. But I promise to try to forgive, even if I must take one baby step at a time. In Jesus' name, amen.

Weekly Watering

◊ **A Light Sprinkling**

1. How can you and I continue to overcome evil with good? To whom must you and I leave ultimate vindication of the world's moral order? (See Romans 12:19 and 1 Thessalonians 4:6.)

2. During this first week, you have taken several significant steps toward forgiving. You have committed your heart to seek to forgive your offenders. That is such an important first step on your path of forgiveness. Read the index cards and repeat yesterday's prayer. You've listed the offenders, their injuries to you, and the debts they owe you. Take a few moments and review the devotions of this past week. Jot down some things you learned that you had never thought about before.

◊ **A Good Long Soaking**

1. Review Monday through Friday's devotional studies, stopping to ponder those lessons most significant to you.

2. Give some attention to how Luke describes Jesus' crucifixion and forgiveness in Luke 23:34. On an index card, write down the prayer Jesus prayed for his enemies. List the ways Jesus' enemies responded to his verbal prayer for them. What do you discover? Insert the card in your Bible.

3. Reflect on Stephen's story as you read Acts 6–7. Make a list of the godly attributes you find in his life and death (for example, his devotion to God, love for his enemies, desire to share his testimony in the final moments of his life, etc.).

4. Make a list of the godly attributes you *possess* in your own life.

5. Make a list of the godly attributes you *desire* in your own life.

6. This week, we have talked about forgiveness as a choice we make. What is your definition of "choice"? Look it up in a dictionary and write down the definition.

7. What are the only two genuine options for responding to an undeserved personal injury?

8. What happens when one person retaliates against another? What does Scripture say about avenging an offender?

9. Why do you think that *revenge, reprisal,* and *retaliation* are the three ugliest words in the English language?

◊ Weekend Feeding

My Father, this week I have studied your Word. I have discovered that you want me to rid my heart of anger and rage and bitterness and resentment. You want me to let go of my human nature's desire for retaliation and revenge. I bring again to you the people who are hurting me now, and who have hurt me in the past. I have committed my heart to forgiving these offenders, Lord, these people who have hurt me so deeply. They have each caused me injury. They each owe me a debt. I have taken the first step, Father, on the long road to forgiving each one of them. I can only follow this path if I know you are walking beside me. Please, Father, keep me in your constant care. Strengthen me as I begin my journey toward forgiveness. I do not expect to complete the journey overnight, Father. But at least I am on the right road, and I promise I will take one step at a time toward complete forgiveness. In your beautiful name, I pray, dear Jesus, amen.

A human's natural response to undeserved pain

> Our privilege as Christians is to know that we are forgiven, and that forgiveness reaches us through Jesus Christ.
>
> Paul Tournier

We saw two things happen during the days that followed the 9/11 tragedies.

First, we heard beautiful stories of forgiveness and love and incredible kindness extended one to another. From strangers across the world, money poured in for 9/11's many victims. Churches overflowed with hurting people who sought spiritual answers to frightening questions about God, pain, death, and terrorism. Most Americans united, reached out to one another, and waved their patriotic flags during those days of disbelief and horror. We heard much about prayer and spiritual things in secular news and society. Together the United States hurt, mourned, helped, and tried to heal.

Some Americans, however, weren't so loving. Old human nature, in its natural form of rage, hate, and vengeance showed its ugly face. Uncrucified "sinful nature," with its "passions and desires" (see Gal. 5:24), resorted to rage—rage that randomly reached out and retaliated against anyone who even slightly resembled the hijackers or Middle-Eastern men.

Balbir Singh Sodhi, the father of three children, was landscaping the yard around his Mesa, Arizona, gas station. A member of the Indian Sikh community, Sodhi wore the traditional long beard and turban. In what was later called a crime of hate and revenge, Francisco Roque shot Sodhi to death.

A man in Queens, New York, was shot in the forehead by a BB gun as he left a temple. He had gone there to pray for the victims of 9/11.

Another man in Fairfax, Virginia, was nearly driven off the road by two vans. He was on his way to donate blood.

Rage-filled Americans firebombed a Hindu temple in New Jersey. A Cleveland, Ohio, man in a fit of rage rammed his car into a mosque. Some Muslims in Washington state were afraid to visit their mosques. The Council on American-Islamic Relationships received more than 300 reports of harassment and abuse during the week that followed 9/11.[1]

Rage and racial hate ruled some people in our society, giving them a taste for blood, for revenge, for violence.

After the 9/11 attack, John Paul II said, "We pray for the victims today, may they rest in peace. And may God show mercy and forgiveness for the authors of this horrible terror attack."

Not many Americans, however, could pray for the forgiveness of the terrorists.

"The human heart revolts at such petitions," writes Alan Cochrum. "Whatever the souls who planned such atrocities deserve, we think, it is not forgiveness or mercy. No, it is something much more elemental—something involving heaving anxiety and heart-stopping terror and long, drawn-out agony."[2]

But what can we expect when our "natural" human emotions take the driver's seat of our heart and mind? Anger, hostility, and violence are natural, predictable responses to raw shocking pain. Should we be surprised? Didn't Paul tell us that before we accept Christ, and become children of God, and receive our "new nature," we are "dead in [our] sins and in the uncircumcision of [our] sinful nature"? (see Col. 2:13). The good news Paul gives us, however, is that "God made you alive with Christ. He forgave us all our sins, having canceled the written code, with its regulations, that was against us and that stood opposed to us; he took it away, nailing it to the cross" (Col. 2:13–14).

You see, a human's natural response to pain is anger, hostility, resentment, rage, bitterness, and the urge to avenge. Only with the mind of Christ—a mind that Christ inhabits—can we desire to genuinely forgive those who hurt us. When forgiveness penetrates our hearts, it dissolves the natural responses of reprisal. Christ's love in our lives blows the battle bugle: love versus hate, forgiveness versus vengeance, hostility versus goodwill. When we choose love, when we choose forgiveness, we win the war.

"As I have loved you," Jesus says, "so you must love one another" (John 13:34). Love, like forgiveness, is a choice we make. The reward for loving and forgiving is a heart full of God's peace. We forgive others because God, through Christ, has so lovingly forgiven us. Love and forgiveness cannot be separated. They form an alliance with each other. They share the same foxhole in the believer's "new nature."

It was Christ's love and forgiveness that helped Stephen pray: *Lord, do not hold this sin against them.*

It was Christ's love and forgiveness that helped Todd Beamer pray: *And forgive us our debts, as we also have forgiven our debtors.*

Jesus told his listeners to forgive those who hurt them. But he went one step further. He told them to love and pray for those who persecute them! Do good to evil doers! (see Luke 6:27–28).

"How unnatural!" Christ's listeners probably recoiled. "Forgiveness is one thing," they might have reacted, "but *love* and *pray* for our enemies? You've got to be kidding, Jesus!"

How revolting were those words from Jesus' lips on the ears of first-century hate-filled avengers! Be ruthlessly honest with yourself. Is it revolting on your ears as well? In your own hurt do you recognize the urge within to avenge, to strike back, to nurse resentment?

During the next three days, you and I will see how Jesus can change an old sinful "natural" nature into a new loving-forgiving nature. We'll see how God can replace our inherited rebellious nature with his own Spirit's nature. We'll watch the amazing transformation as three "natural women" become three of the Lord's "adopted daughters."

Daily Sunlight

℮ Interact with the Gardener

Last week you listed your offenders and you made a commitment to forgive, embarking on your journey. Today, you will concentrate on forgiving one of those offenders.

Turn in your Bible to John 13:34. Read aloud three times the words of Jesus: "As I have loved you, so you must love one another." Now choose one person from your stack of index cards, and, on the back of that card, write down your responses to these three questions:

1. In what ways has Jesus loved me?

2. In what ways can I show love to [name your offender]?

3. In what ways might the love I show to [name your offender] change his or her heart or life? (Take each card and repeat this process.)

℮ Time to Grow

Since my childhood, I have heard the phrase "Do to others as you would have them do to you" (Luke 6:31). Write down how employing this principle might change the way you feel about or relate to your offenders.

Describe what might happen in our world today if everyone applied this principle to an offender.

Read Luke 6:27. Write down the advice Luke gives us regarding love for our enemies.

List the ways you might apply Luke's teaching to your offenders.

℮ **Prayer**

Thank you, Father, that I have the privilege as a Christian to know that you have forgiven me and that forgiveness comes to me through Jesus Christ. I have made the commitment to start on the path of forgiving the offender I am concentrating on today. Please show me, Lord, how my forgiveness for [name your offender] will change my heart and life. How will forgiving this person bring me freedom from bitterness? Lord, I struggle to know how it is possible for me to love, do good to, bless, and pray for this person. I will depend on you, Father, in my journey to forgive [name your offender]. In Jesus' name, I pray, amen.

Nain's nameless woman of the night

> "Two people owed money to a certain moneylender. One owed him five hundred denarii, and the other fifty. Neither of them had the money to pay him back, so he forgave the debts of both. Now which of them will love him more?"
>
> Simon replied, "I suppose the one who had the bigger debt forgiven."
>
> "You have judged correctly," Jesus said.
>
> Luke 7:41–43 TNIV

The nameless woman from Nain heard that Jesus, the Jewish rabbi, was to dine at Simon the Pharisee's home that evening (see Luke 7:36–50). A notoriously sinful woman, she was sought by Nain's men in the darkest hours of their lustiest nights. To satisfy their illicit sexual cravings, they used her and abused her. Then they tossed her aside like yesterday's crumpled newspaper. The whole town knew her tarnished reputation.

The nameless woman from Nain, however, had come to a turning point in her life. She gazed into the mirror of her soul and could not bear her own reflection. She realized her sinfulness. She craved the forgiveness and peace offered by the popular teacher from Nazareth.

She arrives at Simon's house while Jesus is eating there. Surrounded by harsh, critical men, she enters the house and quietly crashes the dinner party. She expects Simon's self-righteous wrath and prepares herself for his verbal, and perhaps physical, abuse.

When she sees Jesus, she darts to him and collapses at his feet and cries. Her actions sketch the scene of her sinful nature. Her hair cleanses Christ's feet as she yearns for him to cleanse her heart. Her eyes ask for the forgiveness her soul so craves. Her tears create puddles of repentance around Jesus' ankles. Her alabaster bottle of perfume, poured on his toes, pays tribute to the power of his future resurrection and to his divine kingship.

She takes the filth from Jesus' feet onto her lips, her hair, her hands (confession). She washes his feet with her tears (repentance). She anoints his feet with her perfumed oil (stating her belief in him, the promised Messiah). She never says a word. But Jesus reads clearly the message of her heart. She wants his nature, a new nature. She wants to become his child.

What does Jesus do? In the midst of Pharisaic criticism, he accepts her confession and takes her filth onto himself. He will pay the penalty for her sin. He accepts her repentant tears, and forgives her innate wrongdoing. He snuffs out her old nature and lights the fire of his spirit in her heart. He accepts her present of perfume and offers her the gift of eternal life. Jesus speaks with the woman's jailer, gives his own life as bail, puts the key in the lock, and personally opens her prison door.

She is no longer the used and abused woman from Nain—nameless, sinful, and scarlet. She reigns as the newly adopted daughter of the King.

While the two gentle hearts come together in divine love and quiet forgiveness, Simon cracks his verbal whip. "How dare this woman of the street—this damsel of disgusting repute—burst into my tent and touch my guest!" Simon shouts.

"If this man were a prophet, he would know who is touching him and what kind of woman she is—that she is a sinner," Simon mumbles (Luke 7:39).

Then Jesus tells Simon a symbolic story (see Luke 7:41–43). He asks Simon an unusual question: "Simon," he said, "Do you see this woman?"

Of course Simon sees this woman! All eyes are focused on her. She's the main attraction in Simon the Pharisee's dining room circus. She is tiptoeing across the tightrope between Simon's fury and Christ's forgiveness.

"I came into your house," Jesus tells Simon. "You did not give me any water for my feet, but she wet my feet with her tears and wiped them with her hair. You did not give me a kiss, but this woman, from the time I entered, has not stopped kissing my feet. You did not put oil on my head, but she has poured perfume on my feet."

Simon had failed to provide society's expected hospitality. He had neglected to perform the ritual of proper host etiquette. He was falling swiftly from the trapeze of propriety, with no safety net beneath him. He'd be the talk of the town. The tail of the donkey. Nain's new inhospitable clown.

Jesus' next line leaves his host limp yet livid. Simon longs to unleash the lions on Jesus.

"Therefore, I tell you," Jesus states, "her many sins have been forgiven—for she loved much."

While Simon blubbers, "Blasphemy!" Jesus looks into his adopted daughter's tired eyes. He tells her that her sins are forgiven, her debt paid in full. She can leave now with a peaceful heart and a brand new nature—her Father's nature (see Luke 7:36–50).

"Your faith has saved you," Jesus says. "Go in peace" (Luke 7:50).

The former sinner from Nain springs to her feet, elated and alive, possessing a new nature and a new name, the name Jesus has given her: The woman who "loved much."

Daily Sunlight

℮ Interact with the Gardener

Read Jesus' story found in Luke 7:41–43. From your stack of index cards, choose the one offender who has hurt you most deeply. This could be an offense that happened recently or long ago. This is the person who has deliberately injured you more than all of the other offenders. This is the person that owes you the greatest debt.

Write the following question on the index card: "Father, [name your offender] has hurt me so deeply. Is it really possible that I can ever forgive my offender?"

@ **Time to Grow**

Paul writes that we "are justified freely by his grace through the redemption that came by Christ Jesus" (Rom. 3:24). In your own words, define *grace*. Write your response on the index card. Now look it up in a dictionary and write down the following question: "Father, you have extended your grace to me. Is it even possible to think I can extend grace to [name of offender listed above]?"

In today's story about the prostitute from Nain, you saw how Jesus forgave the woman of her many sins and renames her "the woman who loved much." Using your imagination, pretend this forgiven woman turns to the dinner party guests who have ridiculed and belittled her. Pretend she tells these men that she has forgiven them. What do you imagine she might say? What sins might she forgive?

Now pretend you are in the same room with your worst offender, the one you listed above. Using your imagination, face that person and tell the offender what sins you want to forgive.

How did the former sinner from Nain—forgiven by God and having forgiven her offenders—leave the dinner party? Again, using your imagination, look at her face: notice the smile on her lips and the sense of peace in her heart. How is it different from the way it was before she was forgiven, before she chose to forgive her offenders?

@ **Prayer**

Father, I bring [name your offender] before you. This offender has hurt me more deeply than the rest. I pray with new commitment that you will show me how to forgive this person. I want the smile and the peace that the Nain prostitute possessed after she was forgiven, and after she forgave her offenders. I am en route to forgiving [name your offender], Lord. I will continue to depend on you to help me. Please show me how my forgiving this person will benefit me and bring me closer to a peaceful heart. In Jesus' name, amen.

Scribbling in the sand

For all have sinned and fall short of the glory of God.

Romans 3:23

Imagine you are a first-century Jew present in the temple courts on the day religious rulers catch and condemn a woman caught in adultery. They use her to put Jesus to the test. Do you see the woman lying on the ground? She is naked, terrified, trembling. She's just been whisked from the arms of her illicit lover. Caught in adultery, Moses' Law bids us to stone her. And him.

"By the way, where is he, the other guilty party?"

But wait! Let's see what Jesus, the rabbi, says. Let's test him. And if he answers wrong, perhaps we'll stone them both.

Look at her. Surrounded by tormentors. Scared. Alone. We smile. She sobs. She's guilty. We're blood-thirsty. She cowers among us—we who condemn her—and she awaits the stone's first blow.

"Teacher," we growl. "We caught this … this woman in the act of adultery! We have witnesses!"

We bark our insults. Her cheeks burn fiery red. We pick up rocks, ready to rip her flesh.

"We're waiting for your word, Jesus. Surely you, the rabbi, the good teacher, will uphold the Law of Moses. Surely this woman must be stoned to death."

"Now what do you say, Jesus? Will you uphold the Law of Moses and let us kill her? Or will you be merciful and let her live?"

We wait. We watch. We wonder.

"You can't win, Jesus, either way you go. We've got you right where we want you—between a rock and a hard place."

But Jesus surprises us. We watch him quietly bend down and write something on the ground.

Then Jesus stands up and faces us all. "If any one of you is without sin, let him be the first to throw a stone at her," he whispers.

Jesus stoops down and continues his writing.

During the penetrating, awkward silence, we can hear a pebble drop. As Margaret Gramatky Alter explains, "Silence, so seldom employed, is a powerful tool of confrontation."[3]

There is no one among us who has not sinned. In those quiet uncomfortable moments that follow, we all stand before Jesus, sinful, naked, trembling, guilty. We all need forgiveness.

One by one, we unclench our fists and drop our stones. And we turn and walk away.

Jesus turns to the embarrassed woman and asks, "Where are they? Has no one condemned you?"

"No one, sir," she says.

"Then neither do I condemn you. Go now and leave your life of sin."

As I imagine that ancient scene, my mind's eye rests on the spot where the sinful woman once stood. And I see flowers grow where weeds once reigned.

Daily Sunlight

@ Interact with the Gardener

Today, let's look at the Bible story you just read about. Reread the story of the adulterous woman in John 8:1–11.

1. In what ways did the teachers of the law and Pharisees try to test Jesus?

2. Why does John tell us that the Pharisees tried to "trap" Jesus (v. 6)?

3. In your opinion, why did Jesus bend down and write on the ground?

4. Although Scripture does not say, what do you think Jesus wrote?

5. What was Jesus' statement to those who wanted to stone the woman?

6. Why did the crowd drop their stones and walk away?

Here are possible answers to questions 1, 4, and 6:

According to Herschel Hobbs, "Jesus could not win with the Pharisees. If he counseled mercy, they could accuse him of condoning her deed. If he agreed that she should be stoned, they could accuse him of being unmerciful."[4]

As Michael Card tells us, "We have not the slightest idea what it was Jesus twice scribbled in the sand. By and large the commentaries have asked the wrong question through the ages. They labor over the content, over what he might have written. They ask 'what' without ever realizing that the real question is 'why.' It was not the content that mattered but why he did it."[5]

Again Card explains, "What Jesus did that morning created a space in time that allowed the angry mob first to cool down, then to hear His word, and finally to think about it, be convicted by it and respond—or not ... Jesus' action created a frame around the silence—the kind of silence in which God speaks to the heart."[6]

@ Time to Grow

1. Pretend that you are having a face-to-face conversation with the newly forgiven adulterous woman. What are three things about God's forgiveness that you most want to tell her?

2. Now pretend you are telling her why she must forgive her accusers—those hate-filled offenders who just dropped their stones. What three things would you tell her?

3. From your index cards, choose another offender who has hurt you. Have an imaginary face-to-face conversation with this person. What are three things about God's forgiveness that you want to tell this person?

4. Now pretend that Jesus is talking face-to-face with you. What are three things Jesus tells you to forgive about your offender?

@ Prayer

Father, thank you for forgiving my many sins. I, like the adulterous woman, am also guilty of sin. Thank you for helping me see more clearly now how my forgiving [name your offender] will bring me peace. I too want to see flowers grow where weeds of bitterness now reign. Pull these bitter weeds from my heart, Lord. Thank you for leading me to make the decision to forgive my offenders. Surely, life is too short and too precious for me to hold resentment in my heart. I want to be free. I want to drop my stones of hate and judgment and forgive my accusers and those people who have hurt me in the past. Please, Lord, keep me from judging others who hurt me. Help me to forgive, Lord. Keep me from picking up and throwing my own rocks of condemnation. In Jesus' name, amen.

To be forgiven is the root; to forgive is the flower

To be forgiven is such a sweetness that honey is tasteless in comparison with it. But yet there is one thing sweeter still, and that is to forgive. As it is more blessed to give than receive, so to forgive is a stage higher in experience than to be forgiven. To be forgiven is the root; to forgive is the flower.

C. H. Spurgeon

The Samaritan woman came to Jacob's well at noon, the hottest hour of the day. Even her stone-hardened heart could no longer bear the townswomen's unkind criticism. She tried to avoid them. Their stares were too harsh, their words too cruel. They judged her. They condemned her. Her tired heart could not tolerate one more torturous treatment.

Men had passed through her life like an assembly line. One minute she was married. The next minute she was divorced and miserable. She lived an empty life, devoid of devotion, her emotions drained to the dregs. She strove to survive, day in and day out. She could not remember the last time she smiled.

Can you identify with this woman? Perhaps you have also been the victim of a husband's rejection or abandonment or divorce. Perhaps you are also attempting to survive each day.

John tells us that Jesus *had* to travel through Samaria, the sinful woman's home town (John 4:4). Most Jews didn't go there. Strong antagonism existed between Jews and Samaritans. One could almost taste the ancient hatred between the two. Jews feared and resented the Samaritans and traveled miles out of the way to avoid their land.

Why did Jesus *have* to travel through Samaria? Because a future missionary waited for him by Jacob's well.

Jesus broke man-made "rules" when he approached the Samaritan woman—rules regarding Jews and Samaritans, men and women, rabbis and sinful women. Society forbade them to speak to each other—let alone drink from the same water cup.

But rules made by men never stopped Jesus. He sat down on a rock and initiated a heart-to-heart conversation with her.

"Will you give me a drink?" he asked as they sat beneath Mount Gerizim—the Samaritan's Jerusalem, their place of worship.

She was surprised. She knew the rules. Even so, she conversed with him about Samaritans and Jews, about the depth of Jacob's well, about where her Samaritan forefathers worshiped. She chased conversational rabbits to avoid the deep ache in her hard heart. But Jesus stopped the chase and challenged her heart. He knew her thirst, her need to drink his living water.

"Go call your husband and come back," Jesus told her.

"I have no husband," she said.

"You've had five husbands. And now you're living with a man who won't marry you."

"So you're a prophet, sir."

"Better than that. I am the Messiah you've been waiting for. And I have brought you living water to drink."

She opened her mouth and accepted his cup of living water. She gulped it down, emptying the cup and overflowing her heart. Years of hate and heaviness drained from her soul.

"Daughter," Jesus started to say, but she was gone. She had jumped to her feet and hit the road. Leaving her precious water pitcher behind, she raced toward town to tell her torturing accusers: "I have found the Messiah! Come with me and meet him for yourselves! Come and taste his living water!"

The reward for her forgiving the townspeople was a heart full of God's peace. And one by one she gathered the hateful, the humiliating, the heinous and hauled them to Jesus. They too needed healing. They followed her—the tricksters, the teasers, the tempters, the torturers. And they discovered that the Messiah's forgiveness was even deeper than Jacob's well. They came, they drank and were never thirsty again.

Forgiven. Free. No longer fretting the past. No longer fearing the future.

They repented and received the gift of God's forgiveness and grace. They made the decision to ask God to change the course of their lives.

Repentance is a choice we make, a reassessment of our life, a reexamination of our future. Repentance is not, according to Frederica Mathewes-Green, a "sterile 'grubbing around in one's soul,' not some masochistic self-humiliation, but a reevaluation leading to action . . . Repentance is the way back to the Father. It is both the door and the path, and there is no other."[7]

To repent means to rethink your life, to reevaluate your present situation. Repentance is the beginning of healing and hope. It is a conscious choice you make to accept God's gracious offer of salvation and to follow Christ.

Sitting by Jacob's well with Jesus, the Samaritan woman reevaluated her life. When she decided to repent, she changed the direction of her life. She placed her feet on a different path. Forgiven and filled with Christ's living water, she fled to forgive those who had abused her. She was bursting to broadcast her newfound faith.

I would imagine that, during the years until her death, the Samaritan woman and the new-faith-filled townswomen traveled together to Jacob's well in the cool of the morning or late in the evening.

"Look here," she might have told them and pointed to the well. "This is where I sat. And, here . . . here is where Jesus sat. And here is the place I drank the living water, the place Messiah forgave me, and I forgave myself."

Daily Sunlight

@ Interact with the Gardener

Let's look more deeply at the story of the Samaritan woman in John 4:1–42. Read it carefully, think about the following questions, and record your thoughts.

Why did Jesus *have* to travel through Samaria (4:4)?

Scripture tells us the woman came to the well about "the sixth hour" (noon). Why did she come during the hottest hour of the day instead of the cool of the morning or evening?

Remember times in your own life when you avoided people or places that were hurtful. Is there a name on one of your index cards that was involved in such a time?

@ Time to Grow

Pretend you are sitting on the edge of Jacob's well with the forgiven Samaritan woman. She tells you she wants to run back to town, forgive all those who have so deeply hurt her, and bring them all to meet Jesus. Write down all the reasons you tell her that forgiving her offenders would be a good idea.

From your stack of index cards, choose an offender who hurts you continually, on a day-to-day basis. This might be your husband, child, mother-in-law, coworker, and so on. This might be someone that you must live or work with, and you must somehow forgive even though the hurt continues day after day. Reread the reasons you just listed for forgiving in your imaginary conversation with the Samaritan woman. Could you use these same reasons to explain why you need to forgive your offender?

How might forgiving this person change you? How might forgiving this offender make it easier for you to live with or work beside this person day after day?

Before we pray, take a few minutes, sit quietly by yourself, and ponder the following statement: "To be forgiven is such a sweetness that honey is tasteless in comparison with it. But yet there is one thing sweeter still, and that is to forgive. As it is more blessed to give than receive, so to forgive is a stage higher in experience than to be forgiven. To be forgiven is the root; to forgive is the flower."[8]

In your opinion, is this statement true? Why?

@ **Prayer**

Lord, thank you for your gift of living water to the Samaritan woman and to me as well. Thank you for forgiving me of all my sins, for making me a new creation filled with your Spirit. Please help me as I continue my journey toward forgiving my offenders just as the Samaritan forgave her offenders. Lord, [name your offender] keeps my heart torn up, my stomach in knots. I must deal with this person's cruel behavior toward me on a day-to-day basis. Just like the Samaritan woman had to live among the hate-filled townspeople, I too must deal regularly with my offender. Show me how to forgive this person who hurts me in continual ways. I pray that one day I can completely forgive [name your offender] just like the woman at Jacob's well completely forgave those who abused her. In Jesus' name, amen.

friday

A father's forgiveness

Forgiveness leapt spontaneously from the father's heart, for indeed it had never been absent from it.

Hannah Whitall Smith

The prostitute of Nain (Tuesday), the adulterous woman (Wednesday), and the Samaritan woman at Jacob's well (Thursday), in their own unique ways, confessed, repented of sins, and received Christ's full forgiveness. Each woman then became God's heir, a legal full-fledged family member. The heavenly Father's forgiveness then covered each woman like a warm security blanket. If one stumbled like a toddler, he picked her up and set her back on her feet. If one forgot who she was, he gently reminded her she was the daughter of the King. If one rebelled like a teenager, he waited by the kitchen window to welcome her home.

The Father's forgiveness is forever for his adopted daughters—past, present, and future. Why would any child want to leave her Father? Why would any child travel into a distant country, far from her Father's home?

The story of the prodigal child has always fascinated me (see Luke 15:11–32). A beloved member of his Father's family, the child rebels, demands his inheritance, and races to the far country. He blows his father's money, wines and dines wily women, and drinks excessively. When he loses all his cash, he asks his "friends" for money.

He ends up groping in the pig pen—hungry, homeless, helpless, hopeless. While eating the pig's food, he remembers his father's house, the warmth, the food.

Scripture tells us he finally comes to his senses. His thoughts drift toward home. He picks up his tired broken body and leaves the pig pen.

He wonders, *Will Dad take me back?* He knows he has broken the rules of society and family when he asked for his inheritance. When he asked for his money, he might as well have said, "Dad, I wish you were dead!"

Back at home his father paces the floor and waits for the familiar figure to walk up the way. One day he sees a certain silhouette against the afternoon sky—skinny, shaky, but he knows it's his son. As the figure gets closer, perhaps he notices his son's hands. They no longer look eighteen, but eighty. Sun-scorched, calloused, cupped in pain. Perhaps he notices his son's legs. Once long and strong, now lean and spindly. The shell of his son walks toward him, head lowered in shame, his lips practicing pleas of pitiful apologies. His son—once dead and now alive. His son—once defiant, now defeated. His son—once haughty, now humbled. His son—coming home at last.

How does the father respond? He runs. The father, so socially poised and proper, raises high his thick long robes and takes off running. Running! The father, overjoyed at the sight of his sorrowful son, gallops like a stallion down the dusty road. Perhaps this Hebrew patriarch even jumps a few fences as he races to his returning colt. The father in this story represents God, our Father. Through this representation, we are shown how God responds to our own coming home. He runs.

Ignoring his son's disheveled appearance, he grabs the grubby kid and covers his face with affectionate kisses. He puts rings on those young ruined hands; sandals on those swollen blistered feet; and he covers his sagging shoulders with a handmade robe. Then he calls to his servant: "Let's throw a backyard barbecue! Bring out the fattened calf!"

The servants are shocked. The neighbors are scandalized. The older brother is bitter. But that doesn't stop the father from flying down the road with his robes flapping behind him. Nor from forgiving his boy and welcoming him back into the family fold.

The father's forgiving love runs. It bolts like a thoroughbred at the starting gate. The boy falls into the arms of his forgiving father with the full assurance of his overflowing acceptance. Sure, the boy did wrong. But the father forgives his son before his son even asks for forgiveness. The son makes his confession, but his father has already forgiven him in advance. He welcomes the boy with open arms.

Was the son's confession needed? No, not to procure the father's forgiveness. The father had already forgiven his son long before the boy came home. Confession was needed to restore reunion and fellowship with the father, not to gain the father's forgiveness.

What does this story say to us today? It assures us that, as adopted daughters in our Father's family, God forgives us our past, present, and future sins. He forgives what we have done; he forgives what we are presently doing; and he forgives our future wrongdoings. When we stray away into our own far countries, when we slide back into our old habits, he waits to welcome us home. Our confession leads to reconciliation and reunion. We can take our place once again by our Father's hearth, in full familial fellowship.

The story shows us something else too. We can choose to trek to the far country if we wish. But, as adopted daughters living far away from our Father's hearth, we will be quite miserable. Our new God-given nature will not let us travel too far, or sin too much, without planting the good seed of guilt in our hearts. Holy Spirit-planted guilt is good guilt— the guilt that guides us home again.

Daily Sunlight

@ Interact with the Gardener

The parable of the lost son (Luke 15:11–32) teaches us the value God the Father places on his spiritual sons and daughters. He offers all his children who go astray a warm welcome home. Family is important to the Father. Throughout his Word, God speaks often about his forgiveness of us and his desire that we forgive others.

Do you have someone in your family who needs your forgiveness? Has a family member hurt you in some way? Perhaps you have already written this offender's name on one of the index cards. If not, do so. The most intimate relationships, particularly those within the family nucleus, are often most vulnerable to hurt. Family is for keeps. Forgiveness and reconciliation are important among family members.

@ Time to Grow

Read the three stories Jesus told about lost things: the lost son in Luke 15:11–32; the lost sheep in Luke 15:1–7; and the lost coin in Luke 15:8–10. How do these three parables help you see how precious you are to God and how important you are to his family?

Consider the following questions about today's study and jot down the first thoughts that come to mind.

1. When the father welcomed home the lost son, how did his older brother react?

2. What did the older brother's attitude reveal about his love for the father?

3. What was the older brother's complaint? How did the father answer him?

4. If you could have an imaginary conversation with the older brother, what would you say to him?

5. Why is it necessary that the older brother forgive the foolish younger brother?

6. How will the older brother's forgiveness change his own relationship with the father?

7. If you decide to forgive the family member who has hurt you, how will your forgiveness change your own relationship to the Father?

@ Prayer

Lord, one by one I am committing myself to forgive those who have hurt me. I pray you will help me forgive those offenders who have hurt me once. Help me to also forgive those who hurt me continually— people I must live with, work with, worship with. I pray especially for the family member I have listed today. I pray I can find peace in my heart through my forgiveness, as well as peace in my family. I rest assured in your love, Lord, confident in the fact that you are beside me in this route to forgiveness. In Jesus' name, amen.

Weekly Watering

◊ **A Light Sprinkling**

1. During Week One, you listed all those people who have hurt you. You made the commitment to forgive them, one by one. This week you examined biblical stories that show how forgiving others will benefit you and change your life and relationship with God. Take a few minutes now and review the names and comments on each index card. On a sheet of paper, write down some of the insights that come to you while reviewing the cards.

2. Pray a one-sentence prayer for each name on each card. (Your prayer might be something like this: "Father, I pray for [name your offender], and I pray you will help me in my journey to forgive. Amen.")

◊ **A Good Long Soaking**

1. Name five things you have learned from this week's devotions. (They can be related to the Bible stories, the scriptures used, or your own notes/thoughts about each day.)

2. Choose at least two of the following verses about forgiveness and answer the question(s) about each.

- Read Romans 5:18–19. What sins need God's forgiveness and why?

- What does God promise you in Ephesians 1:7? How does this verse reassure you in your own walk with the Lord?

- Read Romans 3:23 and explain what this verse means.

- What is the "good, pleasing and perfect will" Paul writes about in Romans 12:2?

- Read John 4:39. What happened when the forgiven Samaritan woman told the townspeople about the Messiah? What was the result of her witness?

- Read Colossians 2:13–14. Describe the difference between our natural sinful nature and our new nature in Christ.

◊ **Weekend Feeding**

Father, I feel I am well on the way to forgiving those people who have hurt me. I understand that forgiveness rarely happens overnight. Forgiving an offender takes time. But I am willing to make the effort, Lord. I no longer want to live with a bitter heart, resentful spirit, or broken relationship. As I reflect on the names of my offenders, as well as on their offenses to me, show me how to pray for each one of them. I yearn for the peace that forgiving these offenses will bring to me.

Thank you, Father, for choosing to forgive me. I do not deserve your forgiveness. I could not work hard enough to "buy" your forgiveness. Nothing I can do will earn your forgiveness. It is already done. Your forgiveness comes to me as a free gift. But forgiving me cost you the life of your son. Help me to be a faithful and forgiving daughter. In Jesus' name, amen.

The little "date palm tree"

> Not to forgive imprisons me in the past and locks out all
> potential for change. I thus yield control to another, my enemy,
> and doom myself to suffer the consequences of the wrong.
>
> Philip Yancey

Have you ever decided not to forgive someone who hurt you? Scripture shows us, through the life of Tamar, that when we decide not to forgive an offender, we are the ones who will suffer the consequences, hurting ourselves and often those we love.

Tamar was King David's beautiful virgin teenage daughter. Her name meant "date palm"—a symbol of victory (Rev. 7:9), rejoicing, success, triumph (John 12:13), and fruitful to a great old age (Ps. 92:14). She was innocent, compassionate, and thoughtful. Like all privileged Hebrew girls, Tamar surely looked forward to a bright future, a good marriage, lots of children and grandchildren, happiness, and contentment.

Tamar trusted her brother Amnon. In fact, Amnon's very name meant "trustworthy." But he was not trustworthy. His overwhelming lust schemed trickery and deception to have her. Amnon pretended to be sick and asked for Tamar to come cook for him, so David sent her to care for him.

Amnon sent his servants away. Tamar cooked his dinner and took it to him. Amnon grabbed Tamar, and she pleaded with him to let her go. She knew that rape destroyed a girl's chances for marriage and children. But Amnon paid no attention to Tamar's cries. After he raped her, he told her to get out of his house. He ordered a personal servant to "get this woman out of here and bolt the door after her" (2 Sam. 13:17).

Tamar wept aloud as she left her brother's house. She tore her beautiful robe—the robe worn only by virgin daughters of the king—and heaped ashes on her head.

The Law of Moses had strict rules about virgins. A woman's virginity was her security. It gave her the right to marry well and be of good moral reputation. Thus, a girl's virginity was protected by her family and those who loved her. "If a man happens to meet a virgin who is not pledged to be married and rapes her and they are discovered, he shall pay the girl's father fifty shekels of silver. He must marry the girl, for he has violated her. He can never divorce her as long as he lives" (Deut. 22:28–29). If a virgin pledged to be married is raped, the man faced death for his act (Deut. 22:25). If a girl claimed to be a virgin, and "no proof of the girl's virginity can be found," she "shall be brought to the door of her father's house and there the men of her town shall stone her to death" (Deut. 22:20–21). A girl's virginity was no small matter. Premarital promiscuity meant her death. Upon her wedding day, after her marriage vows, the new wife must show proof of her virginity. Rape ruined a girl's chances of getting married and having a family.

So when Tamar told her brother Absalom what had happened, he was furious. But Absalom "never said a word to Amnon, either good or bad; he hated Amnon because he had disgraced his sister Tamar" (2 Sam. 13:22). He secretly planned his revenge and took the shattered Tamar into his own home and cared for her.

King David was also furious with his son Amnon, yet he did nothing. He just pretended that the rape never happened. Two years later, seething with hate and desire to avenge, Absalom chose an opportune time and ordered Amnon to be killed. When David learned of Amnon's death, he mourned deeply. Absalom ran away.

Rape. Could any crime against a woman be more cruel than rape? What kind of man devises a scheme to violate and devastate a woman in this wicked way? Only an evil, selfish person is capable of such a crime. Perhaps you or someone you know has been hurt like Tamar through rape or violence. Such a crime seems unforgivable.

Tamar chose not to forgive her half-brother. Who could blame her? Amnon ruined her life, her future. Attractive young Tamar built a dark prison of hate, moved in, and lived there for a lifetime. Once a happy carefree young woman, she died a bitter old woman—sad, alone, isolated.

How was Tamar's health throughout her life? Scripture doesn't tell us. But according to the latest health findings, unforgiveness can cause multiple health problems. "When you hold onto the bitterness for years, it stops you from living your life fully," says Fred Luskin, director of the Stanford University Forgiveness Project. "As it turns out, it wears out your immune system and hurts your heart."[1]

Forgiveness researcher Everett Worthington tells us that "grudges are associated with higher levels of cortisol, a stress hormone, that over time can lead to arterial plaque, which can lead to coronary artery disease."[2] Other health problems associated with grudge-holding unforgiveness include high blood pressure, insomnia, stomachache, clenching and grinding of teeth, depression, stiff muscles, low energy, anxiety, dizziness, headaches, deep sadness, and so on.

For the rest of her life and even after Amnon's death, Tamar harbored deep resentment. Scripture closes the chapter of Tamar's story and life in this sad way: "And Tamar lived in her brother Absalom's house, a desolate woman" (2 Sam. 13:20). She became the very opposite of her promising name.

There is a tiny flower called saxifrage. Sometimes known as a "rock-breaker," it grows secretly in the crevice of strong, solid rocks. It sends down a tiny root in the soil around the rock. Yet, as that root begins to grow, it becomes so strong and so powerful, it can literally crack the rock.[3]

Given enough time, the small roots of bitterness in our own hearts can grow so strong and so powerful, it can destroy our lives. Unlike Tamar, you and I must choose to forgive those offenders that hurt us. We must choose forgiveness over bitterness. Otherwise, we incarcerate our hearts in self-made prisons—dark, deserted, and desolate.

A little bright light, however, shone from Tamar's prison. Three sons and a daughter were born to Absalom before his untimely death. Absalom named his daughter, Tamar, after his sister. Scripture tells us that the new "date palm" grew up and "became a beautiful woman" (2 Sam. 14:27).

Daily Sunlight

☺ Interact with the Gardener

Has anyone ever committed a personal crime against you or someone you love (physical hurt, sexual abuse, rape, etc.)? If so, you can
no doubt understand how Tamar came to hate Amnon. How did you
react to this physical pain/crime? Did you ever decide to forgive your
offender? If so, how did your forgiveness change you? If not, can you
see any results of your unforgiveness? What are they?

☺ Time to Grow

Tamar means "date palm tree." Some symbols of the date palm tree
were victory, rejoicing, success, triumph, and fruitfulness to a great
old age. Do you believe it would have been possible for Tamar to
experience healing and restoration and to live up to her name? Why?
Read the whole story of Tamar and her tragedy (2 Sam. 13:1–14:27).
Does Tamar's story resemble your own? If so, in what ways?

☺ Prayer

*Lord, I hurt from the abuse I have suffered. I harbor unforgiveness in
my heart for my cruel offender, Lord. I do not want my unforgiveness
to destroy my life like unforgiveness destroyed Tamar's life. Through
Tamar's tragic story, I have learned that I must choose to forgive. I
love you, Lord. Help me to forgive. In Jesus' name, amen.*

The decision that still haunts

He that cannot forgive others breaks the bridge over which he himself must pass if he would ever reach heaven; for every one has need to be forgiven.

George Herbert

You and I, like Tamar, can choose not to forgive someone who purposely hurt us. We can choose to hold a grudge against the fellow church member who, through a scam, cheats us out of our retirement, or the coworker who lies about us and keeps us from getting a well-earned promotion. But when we make that choice, we pay a tremendous price.

In his book *In the Freedom and Power of Forgiveness*, John MacArthur writes, "Unforgiveness is a toxin. It poisons the heart and mind with bitterness, distorting one's whole perspective on life. Anger, resentment, and sorrow begin to overshadow and overwhelm the unforgiving person—a kind of soul-pollution that enflames evil appetites and evil emotions."[4]

Like Tamar, Simon Wiesenthal chose anger, resentment, and sorrow over forgiveness. The decision haunted him for the rest of his life. Born in 1908 in Buczacz, Poland, Wiesenthal, an educated Austrian Jew, survived the brutal Nazi concentration camps of World War II. After the war, he dedicated his life to tracking down and prosecuting former Nazi offenders who had organized the imprisonment and persecution of the Jews. He captured the infamous Nazi war criminal, Adolph Eichmann, who in 1960 was transported to Israel, tried, condemned, and executed.

In Poland in 1944, Wiesenthal, an inmate in a Polish concentration camp, worked on the cleanup crew at a makeshift hospital for German soldiers. The hospital was the same building where Wiesenthal had once attended school. As Wiesenthal traveled to the hospital, he passed a cemetery for deceased Germans. He noticed that each German grave had a sunflower on it. In his mind, Wiesenthal contrasted the sunflower-decorated graves of the Nazis with the unmarked mass graves of his fellow Jews. The sight stung him and filled his heart with venom. Surely, his reaction was understandable.

When Wiesenthal arrived at the hospital, a nun took him to the room of a twenty-one-year-old dying Nazi soldier named Karl. One of Hitler's cruel SS men, Karl had been severely injured. Bandages covered Karl's body, including his eyes and head. Barely able to speak, Karl pled with Wiesenthal to listen to him. The young Nazi then confessed his many monstrous war crimes against the Jewish people. He told Wiesenthal about a particular sadistic incident that mercilessly tortured his memory. Karl admitted to setting fire to a building crammed full of Jewish men, women, and children. Ashamed, he told Wiesenthal about one particular family who, with hundreds of others, burned alive that day. The family's smoke-smeared faces burned an image in Karl's mind that haunted him. Karl begged Wiesenthal, the Austrian Jew, to forgive him on behalf of all Jews, for his part in the Nazi's war crimes. Karl wanted to die in peace, forgiven.

In horror, Wiesenthal listened to Karl's story. Although repelled by Karl's confession, he believed its authenticity. He sat patiently by Karl's side as the young German Nazi indicated that he wanted to die in peace, that he had longed to talk about his crime to a Jew and beg his forgiveness.

Karl's confession and apology moved Wiesenthal's heart. But Wiesenthal was unable to forgive the miserable dying man. "At last, I made up my mind and, without a word, I left the room," Wiesenthal said.

He later agonized over his decision. He became troubled by his choice to leave the room in silence, his decision not to forgive the dying Karl. He became obsessed with the question "Ought I to have forgiven him?"

After the war ended, Wiesenthal visited Karl's mother. She confirmed the truthfulness of Karl's confession and the sincerity of his repentance. Wiesenthal spent the rest of his life with the question on his lips: "Ought I to have forgiven him?" He asked his fellow inmates, his friends, his future colleagues, what they would have done. He asked novelists, theologians, lawyers, judges, and other intellectuals—including Protestants, Catholics, and Jews, as well as agnostics and atheists—what they would have done.

Some said Wiesenthal should have forgiven Karl. Others thought he never should have forgiven him. Some interpreted his silence, as he left the room, as a gesture toward forgiveness. Others thought it was a pointed refusal to forgive. Some worried that forgiveness would have been interpreted as a form of "cheap grace." Others worried about the effects a refusal to forgive would bring to Wiesenthal's life.

Wiesenthal refused to forgive Karl for his unspeakable sins against the Jewish race. And his decision haunted him for the rest of his life.[5] How can a Jewish man forgive a German Nazi soldier who helped Hitler exterminate millions of Jewish people? We still see the effects of hatred and prejudice around the world today. How can we possibly forgive those people who murder, rape, rob, and ruin others? Does God really intend for us to forgive them?

Wiesenthal couldn't forgive Karl because the Nazis' crimes were too horrible, too violent. Perhaps he thought that, in order to forgive the Nazis, he would have to condone or excuse their cruel acts. Is there a limit to forgiveness in relation to massive evils and injustice? I believe that no matter how horrible the crimes are, we can still choose to forgive. If we decide not to forgive, then we are left with a poisonous bitterness, like Wiesenthal's, that follows us throughout our lives.

Pulling up weeds of bitterness might take a long time. Remember, forgiveness is a process, a journey. But you and I can start the process with the willful decision to forgive. God will help us along our journey to complete forgiveness, one step and one day at a time.

C. S. Lewis spent an entire lifetime trying to rid his heart of the bitterness he felt for a childhood schoolmaster. As a boy in an English public school, Lewis had a teacher who bullied him and made him miserable. Even as a grown man, he worked hard to forgive this teacher and to rid his heart of bitterness. But he failed, time and time again. Shortly before he died, (Jack) Lewis wrote a letter to his American friend, Mary.

"'Dear Mary,' he began '. . . Do you know, only a few weeks ago I realized suddenly that I had at last forgiven the cruel schoolmaster who so darkened my childhood. I'd been trying to do it for years; and like you, each time I thought I'd done it, I found, after a week or so it all had to be attempted over again. But this time I feel sure it is the real thing . . . Yours, Jack.'"[6]

Johann Christoph Arnold, the author of *Seventy Times Seven,* writes, "Bitterness is more than just a negative outlook on life. It is a sin. To willfully hold on to grudges against another person has a disastrous effect on the soul. It opens the door to evil and leaves us vulnerable to thoughts of murder . . . Bitterness destroys our souls, and it can destroy our bodies as well."[7]

Daily Sunlight

℮ **Interact with the Gardener**

Read the following quote by John MacArthur and write down your thoughts: "Unforgiveness is a toxin. It poisons the heart and mind with bitterness, distorting one's whole perspective on life. Anger, resentment, and sorrow begin to overshadow and overwhelm the unforgiving person—a kind of soul-pollution that enflames evil appetites and evil emotions."

- How is unforgiveness in your life like a toxin or poison?
- How can bitterness poison your heart and mind?
- How can bitterness distort your whole perspective on life?
- Have you ever felt the anger, resentment, and sorrow that accompany unforgiveness? If so, describe how it felt.

- In what ways did it overshadow you and overwhelm you?
- In your opinion, how can unforgiveness enflame evil appetites and evil emotions?

@ Time to Grow

Let's reflect on the sin of bitterness. Did you know that bitterness began in the first garden, the Garden of Eden? Read the following Scriptures and then record your thoughts on the questions below.

- Name God's instruction to Adam in the Garden of Eden. (Gen. 2:15–17)
- What was the couple's sin? (Gen. 3:6)
- What happened immediately after they sinned? (Gen. 3:7)
- In what ways did sin change the first garden? (Gen. 3:17–18)
- How did sin change Adam's vocation? (Gen. 3:19)
- How did Adam and Eve's disobedience bring bitterness to the human race? In what ways did their sin bring spiritual, physical, and social deprivation?
- Use your imagination to answer this question: What kind of relationship might Adam and Eve have had after the Fall? Describe how bitterness might have disrupted their love for each other, their marriage, and their family.

Imagine this scene: God puts cherubim and a flaming sword to separate Adam and Eve from the Garden of Eden. They are no longer allowed to live there (Gen. 3:24). The cherubim and sword represent the barrier that sin brought between sinful man and holy God. Adam and Eve no longer know peace. Do you see how bitterness—toward God and toward each other—abounded in the hearts of this first couple?

☺ **Prayer**

Father, rid my heart of all the toxin and poisons of anger, resentment, and bitterness that unforgiveness brings. I won't allow my unforgiveness for my offenders to poison my heart and mind, or distort my whole perspective on life. I refuse to allow bitterness to overshadow and overwhelm me. I want to say no to evil appetites and evil emotions that the sin of unforgiveness causes.

Please, Lord, knock down that barrier wall of unforgiveness that separates me from my offenders. Help me to realize that my bitterness hurts me far more than it hurts my offender. In Jesus' name I pray, amen.

Tragedy at Tchefuncte River

> Forgiveness is not just a "good idea" or "a nice Christian thing to do." It's an essential of life.
>
> Grace Ketterman and David Hazard

Bitterness most often happens when someone forces us to do something against our will. They control us. The offender might be a controlling spouse who won't allow you to spend time with your family or friends. Or a friend who threatens to reveal a confidence you've shared with her. The offender might even be a kidnapper or a rapist who controls you, takes advantage of you, and hurts you. Debbie Morris experienced a nightmare when two men kidnapped her, raped her, and shot her boyfriend in the head. She learned firsthand how hate and bitterness destroy a life. It almost destroyed her own.

I met thirty-eight-year-old Debbie Morris at a Prison Fellowship Ministry fundraising banquet. A small, gentle, soft-spoken woman, Debbie told me a story that sent chills down my spine.

At age sixteen, Debbie had been a Christian for only two years. On a peaceful night in Madisonville, Louisiana, Debbie and her boyfriend, Mark, parked their car by the Tchefuncte River and sipped milkshakes. They paid little attention to the white pickup truck that pulled up beside them on the isolated riverfront. They sensed no apparent danger. But suddenly, a revolver thrust through the driver's window and pointed at Mark's head. A strong hand jerked Debbie's head back and a voice said, "Don't do anything stupid! We've killed before and we'll kill again." Debbie felt the barrel of a sawed-off shotgun pressed against her left cheek.

"I remember the helpless, sick feeling in my stomach as my whole world went suddenly spinning wildly out of control," Debbie said. "I remember the heart-pounding terror threatening to explode in my chest. I remember mind-clenching panic."

The two men, Robert Willie and Joseph Vaccaro, murderers and escapees from Angola Prison, were high on drugs when they jumped into Mark's T-bird. Then the nightmare began. They drove Debbie and Mark past Bayou Desire on empty roads and into deep pine forests. Across Highway 190, they turned onto Tantilla Ranch Road. They pulled over and hit Mark over the head with a gun and shoved his body into the car trunk. Then Robert Willie brutally raped Debbie.

"Things seemed to be going from bad to worse in a hurry," Debbie said. "I've got to be able to do something, [I thought]. But what? My body felt numb. Exhausted. Yet my mind raced furiously from one imagined scenario to another in search of some workable plan of escape."

After filling the car with gas, the escapees headed toward Florida. Passing the Gulf Shore, Alabama, exit, Joe stopped the car in an isolated clearing. Willie marched Mark off into the woods. Debbie heard the sounds of a struggle, Mark's muffled, frightened voice, and then a gunshot. Willie and Joe came back to the car without Mark.

"I heard their spine-chilling, maniacal laughter followed by a pair of animal-like screams that set me shivering and shaking all over," Debbie recalls. "That's when Willie pulled a big folding knife out of the front pocket of his dirty blue jeans. He opened it up to reveal an ominous-looking blade, at least four inches long. 'I wonder what this would feel like sticking in that pretty skin of yours,' he asked me."

Joe stopped at the Florida Welcome Station and took free samples of orange juice. Debbie had no chance to escape. She worried about Mark. Without warning, Joe jerked the car around and headed west again, back to Louisiana. "We're headin' home now, blondie," Willie told Debbie. "When we get there, we're gonna let you go!"

"Please!" Debbie panicked and cried. "You have to let me go!"

"Stop that! Stop that cryin' now!" Joe demanded. "I can't stand it when a girl cries. Just stop it!"

"I can't help it," Debbie sobbed. "Let me go! Please!"

Vaccaro grew visibly upset. "Shut up, girl," he screamed. "I said, shut up!"

At that, Vaccaro lashed out with his right arm. With his right fist still gripping the stock of his pistol, he punched Debbie in the chest with the back of his hand. Hard.

"The sudden blow knocked the air out of me," Debbie said. "It reminded me how helplessly unpredictable my situation truly was ... My captors were still very much in control. 'What am I going to do, Lord?' Debbie prayed. 'You have got to help me get away!'"

Already Debbie intensely hated her kidnappers, but her ordeal was far from over.

Daily Sunlight

ℰ Interact with the Gardener

Have you ever been put in a helplessly unpredictable situation where you felt another person's ruthless control? If not, try to imagine how you would answer these questions if you had experienced Debbie Morris's nightmare. How did you deal with the incident? What did you do to ensure your survival? How did you feel toward your offender(s)? Did you ever make the choice to forgive them? How? Why?

ℰ Time to Grow

Think about the incident you just described. As you reflect on your own situation, why do you think "forgiveness is not just a good idea or a nice Christian thing to do," but "an essential of life"?

Describe what happens to a Christian woman when she refuses to forgive someone who has hurt her in a cruel physical way. What physical health problems might she suffer?

Perhaps you have never encountered a situation like Debbie's. Do you know of family members or friends who have had a similar experience? How did they handle it? Did they eventually forgive their offenders?

@ **Prayer**

Father, I am discovering that the more violent the crime against me, the harder it is to forgive. Show me what to do with the anger and bitterness I feel toward my offender. Please give me special comfort, for I have suffered pain at the hands of cruel others. I wonder, Lord, how you were able to so completely forgive those cruel people who crucified you. I have such a hard time with forgiving a cruel offender. I pray this prayer in your precious name, dear Jesus, amen.

thursday

The nightmare

> None of us can afford to pay [the costs of unforgiveness]
> because they mean forfeiting the peace, stability, and
> soundness of our inner being.
>
> Grace Ketterman and David Hazard

Still in the deadly grip of the kidnappers, Debbie remembers, "I'd never in my life felt the kind of hatred I felt right then. I wanted to see Robert Willie rot in hell for what he had done to Mark and to me."

At some point that afternoon, Vaccaro told Debbie, "You sure are nicer than our last girlfriend." Then he added: "I sure hope what happened to our last girlfriend don't happen to you! Everythin' was fine and the next thing I knowed she was lying there ... dead."

As Debbie recalls, "It was like Vaccaro was having some kind of flashback and seeing it all in his mind. It was giving me the chills."

"She was all cut up and stabbed in the chest. It was terrible."

"Shut up!" Willie shouted. Vaccaro got quiet. They headed north toward Franklinton and stopped the car. "Get in the back seat," Willie ordered Debbie. "And take off your clothes!" Again, Willie raped Debbie. Debbie prayed, "Please God, you gotta help me get out of here alive!" She wondered when the nightmare would end.

"We gotta find us some more drugs," Willie said. They decided to try to find an old friend, drug dealer Tommy Holden. After hours of searching that afternoon on Fitzsimmons Road, Vaccaro finally spotted Tommy. They flagged him down. They drove to Holden's cockroach-infested trailer in the middle of nowhere, and Debbie watched the three of them smoke pot and drink beer. Debbie prayed for a way to escape and begged them to let her go. The emotional stress and two days without sleep had caused Debbie to lose any hope of an escape.

"Willie says we can't let you go until I have sex with you," Vaccaro told Debbie. "He doesn't want to be the only one." For the third time, Debbie was violently raped.

"What are y'all planning to do?" Holden asked Willie.

"You askin' me what we need to do?" Willie replied. "I'm sayin' we lock her in the trunk and set the car on fire!"

Debbie remembers, "When I heard that, I experienced a split second of absolute terror. I couldn't imagine a more terrible fate than being burned alive while locked in the trunk of a car."

For some insane reason, however, the two drugged men decided to let Debbie out of the car near her Madisonville home. "They stopped and let me out near the cemetery at the outskirts of town," Debbie said. "I couldn't believe they were letting me go. I thought to myself, *They are going to pull up beside me any minute, and drag me back in the car. Or they are going to let me get a little ways down the road so they can run me down and kill me with the car.*"

Debbie flinched when she heard tires squeal as the car behind her took off and roared toward her. *Let them run me down,* Debbie thought. *At least it will be over with.* She didn't look back. She tensed for the impact. But, to her amazement, the car accelerated right on past her.

They're going to stop any second, Debbie thought. But they didn't. Instead, the car disappeared around the curve and continued out of sight. Willie and Vaccaro had, for some reason, released Debbie. She kept walking until she reached town.

During the long ordeal, Debbie's family begged the police to look for the missing teenager. But the police brushed them off. "This kind of thing happens all the time. She'll probably be home soon," they said. The teen had to have been gone for seventy-two hours before they could officially list Debbie as "missing," and put out an all-points bulletin.

After Debbie returned home, she worked with police in their search for Willie and Vaccaro. Debbie led the police to the place where they had left Mark. Willie and Vaccaro had done unspeakable things to Mark before they shot him. Debbie and the police found Mark. He had a gunshot wound to his head. He was barely conscious, but he was alive!

Over the years, Mark would recover from the attack, but he would need a lifetime of therapy to learn again how to do life's most simple tasks.

Police finally found and arrested Willie and Vaccaro somewhere in Arkansas. For his crimes, Joseph Vaccaro was imprisoned. Robert Willie later died in the electric chair. Debbie also gave detectives the information she had heard from Willie and Vaccaro. She told them about their "last girlfriend," the young woman they claimed to have killed. Police discovered the victim's name was Faith Hathaway. With Debbie's help, police later found Faith's decomposing body. Planning to also kill Debbie, Willie had taken Debbie to the same place where he had earlier killed the young woman. Only God knows why Willie didn't.

Daily Sunlight

℮ Interact with the Gardener

Debbie admits, "I'd never in my life felt the kind of hatred I felt right then. I wanted to see Robert Willie rot in hell for what he had done to Mark and to me." Have you ever felt this degree of hatred toward somebody? If so, what did this intense hatred do to your body, mind, emotions, and soul? How did your hatred interfere with your relationship to others and to God? Can you identify with Debbie and with her hatred for the two men who kidnapped, raped, and took control of her? In what ways?

Name some of the costs of unforgiveness you have personally experienced. In what ways did your unforgiveness forfeit the peace, stability, and soundness of your inner being?

In what ways did unforgiveness affect your physical health?

℮ **Time to Grow**

Take a moment to read Colossians 3:13. In this verse, Paul urges you and me to "bear with each other and forgive whatever grievances you may have against one another. Forgive as the Lord forgave you." In your opinion, what does Paul mean when he writes "whatever grievances you may have"? Do you know of any grievances that are unforgivable?

Read and reflect on Mark 11:25. Jesus says, "And when you stand praying, if you hold anything against anyone, forgive him, so that your Father in heaven may forgive you your sins." How does unforgiveness toward another person interrupt our prayers and fellowship with Christ? Has unforgiveness for one of your offenders ever interrupted your prayer and fellowship with Christ? If so, describe the ways.

℮ **Prayer**

My Father, keep from my heart the sin of unforgiveness. Help me to forgive even those who deeply hurt me. I pray in Jesus' precious name, amen.

Forgiving the rapist

> While the biblical practice of forgiveness is usually preached as
> a Christian obligation, social scientists are discovering that
> forgiveness may help lead to victims' emotional and even
> physical healing and wholeness.
>
> Gary Thomas

In spite of her belief in Jesus Christ, the support of her family and
church, Debbie's life began to deteriorate. She quit high school. She
moved around the country working odd jobs for meager living expenses
and developed such a serious drinking problem that she experienced
alcoholic blackouts. Debbie's mother finally convinced Debbie to get
professional help. She checked herself into a thirty-day treatment program at a Baton Rouge hospital, and with help, Debbie's messed-up life
began to change. But before Debbie could be completely healed, she
knew she had some hard work to do. She had to forgive Robert Willie.

After Willie's execution, Debbie felt numb. "It's over at last," she told
herself. But she felt spiritually confused. "As a kid and as a young
teenager I believed in God," she said. "I trusted him. And then he let me
down. Okay, maybe he saved me and gave me another chance at life.
But what about all the pain and unhappiness I've gone through . . .
where was the Almighty in all that? If he really, truly loved me like the
Bible claims, why would he let me go through all the heartache and
suffering?"

Debbie was angry—at herself for her lapse into a life of promiscuity and alcohol following the kidnapping, at Willie and Vaccaro for the
suffering they had caused, and at God for allowing her this tragedy.

Over time, Debbie made peace with God. And she forgave herself. It wasn't easy, but she finally went to her knees and asked God to forgive her for her attitude and for the sinful mistakes she had made after the kidnapping.

"As I came to know and feel God's forgiveness, it was suddenly easy to forgive myself," she said. "And what a new and incredible sense of freedom I felt!"

In order to find Christ's perfect peace, Debbie knew she had to forgive Robert Willie. "My reluctance to forgive was like a darkness inside, a barrier that barred joy and love and so many good things from my life," she said. "I couldn't begin to articulate it at the time, but I knew I had to forgive him—not for his sake, but for mine. Until I did, there was no escaping the hold his evil had on my life. Until I forgave him, real healing couldn't begin."

Debbie thought her anger for Robert Willie, as well as her emotional wounds, would subside, and even heal, after Robert Willie was executed for his murder of Faith Hathaway. She realized, however, that "no punishment—not even the ultimate punishment, the ultimate justice [Willie's execution]—could ever heal all the wounds."

For a long time, Debbie walked the hard road toward forgiveness. An unforgiving spirit, however, festered within her for many years. How in the world could she ever forgive Robert Willie for what he had done to her, for how he had ruined her young life, for what he had done to her boyfriend, for the pain he had caused her family? Forgiveness seemed impossible. Yet, as a Christian believer, she knew she had to forgive him.

For Debbie, forgiveness took time. It was a long, painful process. But God walked with her throughout the journey. In time, she completely forgave Robert Willie and Joseph Vaccaro for their unspeakable crimes against her.

"People often ask me how can you forgive someone who has done something so terrible?" Debbie said. "The word 'forgive' means to give something the other person doesn't deserve. God has modeled this for us by offering anyone—even those who are completely undeserving—forgiveness through his only Son."

Robert Willie certainly didn't deserve Debbie's forgiveness. "He didn't deserve it," she said. "He didn't benefit from it—he was executed." Debbie admits, "I in no way absolved him of his responsibility for what he did to me. He has to answer for that. And he did. But I do know that until [I forgave them], Robert Willie and Joseph Vaccaro were behind bars, but I was the one in prison. My refusal to forgive him always meant that I held on to all my Robert Willie-related stuff—my pain, my shame, my self-pity. That's what I gave up in forgiving him. And it wasn't until I did that that real healing could begin. I was the one who gained."[8]

Forgiving Willie and Vaccaro changed Debbie's life. God rewarded Debbie with a heart full of his peace. A devoted Christian woman, she is now happily married and the mother of two young children. She works as a public school special education teacher with a particular concern for troubled students considered most at-risk for future involvement in violence and crime. She also travels the country and tells her remarkable story of Jesus Christ and his power of forgiveness.

Daily Sunlight

℮ Interact with the Gardener

After reading Debbie's story, take a few minutes to reflect on it and pen your thoughts and answers to the following questions.

After her abduction, Debbie asked God some serious questions. What were they? Have you ever asked God those kinds of questions? If you could talk personally with Debbie from your own experience with unforgiveness, how would you answer her questions?

How did unforgiveness affect Debbie's life? Has unforgiveness ever affected you in the same or similar way? Please describe.

@ **Time to Grow**

How did Debbie define the word *forgive?* How would you define it?

What did Debbie give up when she decided to forgive Robert Willie and Joseph Vaccaro? What will you give up when you forgive your offender(s)?

What are some social scientists discovering about forgiveness and a person's health?

@ **Prayer**

Father, I pray for Debbie, and I pray for myself. We have both known the hurt of another's force and control. Forgiveness in these types of situations seems impossible, Lord. But, I know with your help, forgiveness can happen. Even after a trauma as terrible as Debbie's. Walk with me, Lord, as I continue my own journey on the road of complete forgiveness. In Jesus' name, amen.

Weekly Watering

◊ A Light Sprinkling

During the past three weeks, we have studied the true meaning of forgiveness. We have also examined what forgiveness means— personally, spiritually, and relationally. During Week One, you learned that forgiveness is a choice that you can make. It's an act of your will to forgive someone who has hurt you. By the end of Week One, you had a stack of index cards, each one listing the name of one of your offenders. You made the decision to forgive each offender on your list.

During Week Two, we watched Jesus forgive a Samaritan woman at Jacob's well, a prostitute at Simon's dinner party, an adulterous woman, and a rebellious son. We learned that God chose to forgive you and me, and how he chose to do it—through his son, Jesus Christ.

During Week Three, we saw the results of unforgiveness. We watched weeds of hatred and bitterness grow in victims' hearts. We also saw how the act of deliberate forgiveness changed a victim's life, erased the hate, eased the bitterness. We learned the reasons why we must choose to forgive others.

1. I invite you to read the names and your comments on each of your index cards. You may want to add the names of other offenders to your index cards—one offender to each card. No

doubt, during this study, you've thought of many more people you'd like to forgive. No matter how small the offense, list these offenders on your cards. The important thing is that you have chosen to forgive these offenders. You have made the difficult decision to release them from the debts they owe you.

2. Ask God to help you commit to the rest of the forgiveness journey as you travel toward complete forgiveness. It will be good for your heart as well as your spirit.

◊ A Good Long Soaking

Let's talk for a moment about heart-health. Let me tell you about Linda Marra, age twenty-eight. In 1987 her father was bludgeoned to death. For the next sixteen years, Linda suffered from unforgiveness for her father's killer. During this time, her hair turned gray, she suffered from insomnia, her neck grew so stiff she sometimes couldn't drive. Linda wore a mouthpiece to prevent grinding down her teeth. She took various antidepressants. Nothing seemed to help.

"I felt like I was in a hole and I couldn't dig myself out," she recalls.

One day Linda woke up at 2 a.m., fell to her knees and prayed. She begged for God's help. Two weeks later, she began to read her Bible. While reading the book of Job, Linda, then forty-four years old, forgave the man who killed her father.

She felt release from resentment, and her ailments disappeared.

As Helena Oliviero stated, "Marra's case provides testament to what researchers have discovered: Forgiveness is good for the heart—literally and figuratively."[9]

1. Have you had health problems because you held a grudge? Has holding on to resentment caused you physical distress? If so, describe.

2. Name at least three insights that have become clearer to you because you worked through the past three weeks' Bible studies. List them and describe how you would explain each to someone else.

3. Now, back to the index cards. Arrange your stack one by one on a table. You should be able to see all of them at once. Examine each offender. Ask yourself the following questions as you read each card, and write your answer on the back of the card.

   • What is keeping me from forgiving [name your offender]?

   • What level of hate or bitterness do I feel for this particular person, and why? (Measure this on a scale from one to ten—with ten being the highest hate rating.)

   • If I decide not to complete the forgiveness process, what pain must I live with? How will my unforgiveness affect my life, my health, my relationship with God and with others?

   • If I decide to complete the forgiveness process and completely forgive this person, how will my complete forgiveness benefit my life, my health, my relationship with God and with others?

4. Over the next two weeks, we will examine ten popular myths about forgiveness. These myths hold no seed of truth whatsoever, yet they continue to confuse us and keep us from forgiving our offenders. As you work through the Bible studies during the next two weeks, keep the index cards in front of you. On each card, list the myth(s) that keep you from forgiving each particular offender.

5. Before you pray, let's spend some time in God's Word.

   • List the fifteen "acts of the sinful nature" as stated in Galatians 5:19–21.

   • List the nine "fruit of the Spirit" as named in Galatians 5:22–23. Give a brief definition of each one. Which fruit of the Spirit are in your own life?

   • Paul tells us in Galatians 5:25 to "live by the Spirit," and "keep in step with the Spirit." In your opinion what does he mean? How can you apply Paul's advice to your own life?

◊ Weekend Feeding

Father, I have placed the names of my offenders before me. Please help me to understand what keeps me from forgiving each offender. Release me from the hate and bitterness I feel for each person. Keep me from the sin of unforgiveness and the bitterness it brings my soul. Surely, Father, the price of unforgiveness is too high. I cannot afford to keep unforgiveness in my life. I pray that as I move forward through the next two weeks, you'll help me to distinguish truth from myth. And thank you forever, Lord, for reaching down to me, and forgiving my sins. In Jesus' name I pray, amen.

overcoming the myths
of *forgiveness*

Exposing the Myths

Exposing More Myths

Myth 1: forgiving means the offender didn't really hurt you

Forgiveness is not denying the reality of evil; in fact, forgiveness begins by recognizing evil in all of its horror.

John Claypool

It is no simple task to debunk the myths and lies that prevent us from experiencing forgiveness. Some of these myths we learned as children. Others we have heard over and over throughout our lifetimes. These myths are often subtle and their hold on us can be difficult to break.

Does forgiving negate the massive amount of pain the offender has brought us? Can we forgive an offender and still acknowledge that we are deeply hurt? In fact, the reason we choose to forgive is primarily because the offender intentionally wounded or wronged us. If the person did us no harm, or if the person hurt us accidentally, we wouldn't need to forgive.

Debbie Morris forgave Robert Willie for kidnapping and raping her. But her forgiveness did not cancel out his evil actions. Willie purposely hurt Debbie. He caused her years of pain.

Todd Beamer forgave the 9/11 terrorists who hijacked and crashed his plane. The terrorists did hurt and kill Todd, as well as thousands of other people. Todd's forgiveness didn't undo their evil deeds.

Missy Jenkins has a story of forgiveness that is remarkable. A Christian teenager, Missy loved the Lord. She gathered with her Christian friends each morning at school to pray.

On the morning of December 1, 1997, Missy, a sophomore at Heath High School in Paducah, Kentucky, dressed early and went to school. As usual, she and her Christian friends met before classes began and prayed. But when they said their final "amen," something horrible happened. And it would forever change Missy's life.

At 7:45 that morning, fourteen-year-old classmate Michael Carneal walked up to the prayer group. The students knew him, but they never expected the evil he planned to commit. In his backpack, Michael carried a .22 Ruger semiautomatic pistol. Wrapped in a blanket, he carried four rifles. For no apparent reason, he pulled out the pistol and fired eleven shots into the student prayer group.[1]

By the time he stopped shooting, he had killed three of Missy's friends: Kayce Steger, Jessica James, and Nicole Hadley. He had seriously injured five other students. One of the bullets blasted into Missy's left shoulder and severely damaged her spinal cord. The injury paralyzed Missy from her waist down. Her doctors at Lourdes Hospital told Missy and her family that she would never walk again and would spend the rest of her life in a wheelchair. She would also need extensive physical therapy.

Heath High School principal, Bill Bond, described Michael as a boy who "had been teased all his life." He told reporters after the shooting that Michael felt powerless, that students described him as small and emotionally immature. Bond said Michael "just struck out in anger at the world."[2]

The courts charged Michael as an adult with three counts of murder and five counts of attempted murder. But, as a Christian, Missy knew she could not live with unforgiveness and hate in her heart.

Missy Jenkins chose to forgive the classmate who shot her and paralyzed her young body. "Michael took so much from so many that day. It's hard to realize I may never walk—or dance—again," she said.

Her forgiveness didn't mean that her classmate, Michael Carneal, didn't hurt her. She chose to forgive him because he did hurt her. "I believe hating him is wasted emotion," she says. "I know it isn't what Jesus would do ... Besides, hating Michael won't make me walk or bring my schoolmates—Kayce, Jessica, and Nicole—back to life."

Instead of hating Michael, Missy pities him. "I do feel sorry for Michael," Missy admits. "Unlike him, I can get on with my life . . . I'm not mad at him. I can forgive him."

Michael faced judge and jury—and will one day face God—for what he did. But the moment Missy chose to forgive Michael, she found freedom from prison, freedom from the bars of bitterness that could have incarcerated her for a lifetime.[3]

Daily Sunlight

@ Interact with the Gardener

As you examine your index cards of current and past offenders, is the myth "forgiving means the offender didn't really hurt you" keeping you from forgiving any one of them? If so, make a note of this myth on the back of the card. This is the person that needs your forgiveness today.

Know that your forgiving this offender does not negate the massive amount of pain that person has brought you. In fact, the reason you have chosen to forgive is primarily because this offender intentionally wounded or wronged you. If the person did you no harm, or if the person hurt you accidentally, you wouldn't need to forgive.

- Do you agree?
- Why or why not?
- What is the difference between accidental hurt and intended hurt?
- Which hurt needs your forgiveness and why?

@ Time to Grow

Read Ephesians 1:7–8. In light of this verse, why should you forgive someone who deeply hurts you, or who hurts someone you love?

What did you learn about *intentional* hurt and *accidental* hurt? Which hurt needs your forgiveness? Which hurt needs no forgiveness?

Why does forgiveness begin by recognizing evil in all of its horror? Why is this statement true? How does this statement help you to forgive your offender?

@ Prayer

Father, help me to understand that forgiving my offender does not mean that the offender didn't really hurt me. Show me clearly that the main reason I must choose to forgive is the hurt inflicted upon me. Please, Lord, help me forgive my offenders even though they meant to hurt me. Lord, I forgive [name your offender] as an act of my will. I pray that, in time, you will give me the "feelings of forgiveness" for this offender. In Jesus' name I pray, amen.

Myth 2: forgiving means you condone or excuse the offender's hurtful act

> Forgiveness is a redemptive response to having been wronged and wounded . . . Only those who have wronged and wounded us are candidates for forgiveness. If they injure us accidentally, we excuse them. We only forgive the ones we blame.
>
> Lewis B. Smedes

Have you ever put your trust into someone who betrayed you, lied to you, or deceived you? Did you try to rationalize the offense? Did someone you confided in try to excuse or dismiss the person's actions? Did they say something like, "Oh, it's no big deal. Get over it!" Or, "You're carrying your feelings on your sleeve. Don't let it bother you." Or, "He or she didn't mean to hurt you. Just overlook it." Or, "They were drunk. They didn't mean to hurt you."

The plain truth is that forgiving people does not condone or excuse their crimes (or insults, or lies, or betrayals, or verbal abuses, and so on). It does not brush the hurt aside like you would dismiss an accident or mistake. In the case of accident or mistake, we don't need to forgive. Forgiveness is not even an issue then.

We choose to forgive only those offenders who purposely wrong us and wound us, those who legitimately carry the blame for our pain.

We *excuse* a man if a severe heart attack makes him crash his SUV into our family car, killing our loved ones. His crime was unintentional. Our hurt is deep and devastating, but we cannot hold him responsible.

He too is a victim. In these cases, we reach out and minister to him and his family even as we cry our own tears of grief.

But we are called to *forgive* a man who drinks until he's drunk and then smashes his SUV into our family car. We hold him responsible for his irresponsible behavior of drinking and driving. We work with the courts to keep him off the streets until he stops drinking and driving. He needs help as well as punishment. We don't just slap his hand, excuse him for his drunkenness, and then release him to do the same thing again.

A heart attack-caused crash is an accident. It could happen to anyone. We must excuse it. But a crash caused by a drunken stupor is a crime. We must forgive it, but, at the same time, we must try to prevent it from ever happening again.

We grow understandably upset when a deliberate crime is treated like an accident. Justice means the offender must face an *accuser* not an *excuser*. An entire nation rose up against Russell Yates when he excused his wife, Andrea, from murdering their five children. She plunged each one headfirst in a bathtub full of water and drowned all five youngsters.

"She's a victim; she's not a criminal," Russell argued. "She needs treatment. She doesn't need punishment."[4] After his statement, some people wanted to put *him* on trial with her! No doubt, Andrea Yates did need treatment. But for her crime, she also needed imprisonment.

For drowning her five young children, a Houston, Texas, jury convicted thirty-seven-year-old Andrea Yates on two counts of murder—a minimum of forty years in jail. Russell believed the jurors ignored overwhelming evidence that Andrea was insane. He asked that his wife be excused, released from the blame of his children's death.

"Her heart was good, and her mind was bad. To me, as outrageous as it sounds, I don't think she needs forgiveness, she needs compassion," stated Russell.[5] The jury, however, believed the deaths caused by Andrea are not so easily excused. They had not been convinced that Andrea Yates is psychotic.

Her five children were buried at a combined funeral service on June 27, 2001. More than three hundred mourners gathered at the Clear Lake Church of Christ in Houston, Texas. During the eulogy, Russell Yates stood beside each small casket, and he told the mourners about each one. A happy, smiling picture of each child was shown on a projector screen while he talked.

"I can't possibly tell you everything there is to know about each one of them," he said. "But I can give you a glimpse of who they were. Six-month-old Mary was the princess of the family." He described three-year-old Paul as well-behaved, two-year-old Luke as a rule-challenger, and five-year-old John as having a great smile. Noah, seven years old, was described as intelligent, independent, and a bug-lover. Then he turned to baby Mary, dressed in pink: "Sorry I didn't get to see you grow up. I love you. Rest in peace."

Russell placed a special blanket next to each little body, and the coffins were closed for the final time. Mr. Yates touched each one and wept as officials slowly wheeled the small coffins to a nearby cemetery.[6]

You can choose to forgive an offender and still recognize the brutality of the act.

Daily Sunlight

⊘ Interact with the Gardener

Let's spend a few minutes in the Word.

Read Ephesians 2:12–13. In your opinion, what is meant by "the blood of Christ"?

Read Ephesians 4:18. In your own words, what do you think Paul means by "the hardening of their hearts"?

Read 2 Corinthians 5:19–21. Describe in your own words what Paul means by the phrase "be reconciled to God."

How can a person do that?

Pause and say a prayer for at least one of your offenders. Ask God to "soften" the offender's heart, to show that person (if that person is not a believer) how to be reconciled with God through Jesus Christ.

@ **Time to Grow**

Let's do a quick word study: Using a dictionary, look up the word *condone* and write down the meaning. (Some synonyms for *condone* in this setting are to overlook the offense, to disregard or ignore it, to close your eyes to the hurt someone caused you.)

Now look up the word *excuse* and write down the meaning. (Some synonyms for *excuse* in this setting are to justify or reason away the offense, to try to explain or rationalize why the offender hurt you, and to pretend the offense didn't happen or wasn't that serious.)

Now look through your index cards, and note which of your offenders you are struggling to forgive. Is it because you think that if you forgive the offender, you'll be condoning or excusing the crime against you? If so, consider this statement by Lewis Smedes: "Forgiveness is a redemptive response to having been wronged and wounded ... Only those who have wronged and wounded us are candidates for forgiveness. If they injure us accidentally, we excuse them. We only forgive the ones we blame."[7]

@ **Prayer**

Father, help me to recognize the difference between an accident and an intentional hurt. Keep me from the temptation to rationalize or justify my offender's hurting me. Help me to forgive them and never just overlook or disregard their offenses. Please show me how to forgive someone who deliberately causes my wounds. I pray in Jesus' name, amen.

Myth 3:
before forgiving, you must first understand why the offender hurt you

> When I was explaining to my daughter that Graham and the
> boys had been killed, we agreed that we would forgive those
> who did it. And I can say from my own experience that
> forgiveness brings healing.
>
> Gladys Staine

Our human minds yearn to understand why some people cause others such pain. We want to make all the confusing puzzle pieces fit before we can forgive the offender and put the tragedy behind us.

We may never understand the cruel actions of people like Hitler or Stalin or Eichmann or Bin Laden or Michael Carneal or Timothy McVeigh.

McVeigh, the twenty-seven-year-old who bombed Oklahoma City's Alfred P. Murrah Federal Building on April 19, 1995, seemed like the boy next door, an average American guy. While fighting for our country, the government had even awarded this Gulf War veteran the Bronze Star. McVeigh's lawyer, Richard Burr, couldn't figure out why McVeigh coldly killed 168 people in the Oklahoma City bombing. Burr represented McVeigh for five years. He came to know McVeigh well during the trial. Burr insists McVeigh is not the "robotic killer hated by millions. He is a full, real human being with a full range of emotions," Burr claims.

But McVeigh left even Burr scratching his head and wondering why. "You would not expect such a human being to do something like this. That's what's so baffling and maddening to people trying to understand this."[8]

We cannot understand McVeigh's reasons any more than we can figure out why eleven boys, ranging in ages from fifteen to seventeen, walked down the street in Aterson, New Jersey, and hit, kicked, and beat every person in their path. For no apparent reason, they "punched a Puerto Rican in the face," and "punched a Bengali boy in the face." They also attacked a Hispanic student and a local delivery man.

Then they saw Hector Robles, a forty-two-year-old homeless Puerto Rican they described as a "bummy-looking guy." While forty other teens watched, they kicked and stomped Mr. Robles, and threw beer bottles at him.

"They were beating him and kicking him like he was a dog," said one witness. Their repeated blows ruptured Mr. Robles's spleen. Doctors declared him dead at a nearby hospital. No one could understand the boys' murderous actions.

"We're not accustomed to having children killing people," said Bob Grant, spokesman for Mayor Marty Barnes. Police arrested the boys and charged them with murder.[9]

We will never understand the reasons for child molestation or rape or spousal abuse or mutilation or murder. How does this affect our decision to forgive? Our forgiveness may do nothing to help the offender who will answer to God. But our forgiveness will make a world of difference in our lives. As Christian women, forgiveness proves the only way to achieve freedom of spirit and emotional healing.

Missionaries Graham and Gladys Staines worked for thirty-four years with lepers in India. Since leprosy sufferers were rejected by society, the Staines tried to "show them love and acceptance." That "makes a huge difference in their healing," Gladys admits, "the fact that we love them, accept them and touch them."

On January 23, 1999, Graham and his sons, Philip, age ten, and Timothy, age eight, were asleep in a vehicle in the village of Manoharpur, Orissa. They were tired. They had been holding open air meetings in the village. A group of militant Hindus walked up, doused the vehicle with gasoline, and set it on fire. Then they prevented Graham and his sons from escaping. Surely, we will never understand the cold, calculating hearts that torture and murder.

Gladys buried her husband and sons in the leprosy home's cemetery. She chose to continue her work in India, even at the risk of death. She also chose to forgive the militant Hindus who killed her husband and two sons.

Like Gladys, you and I can choose to forgive a person who hurts us even though we will never understand the reasons for the monstrous acts.

Daily Sunlight

@ Interact with the Gardener

How did God speak to you today as you read about missionaries Graham and Gladys Staines?

If you had been Gladys, describe the struggle you would have felt in deciding whether or not to stay and continue the ministry to India's lepers.

If you could speak personally with Gladys Staines, what would you want to tell her?

@ Time to Grow

"Our human minds yearn to understand why some people cause other people pain. We want to make all the confusing puzzle pieces fit before we can forgive and put the tragedy behind us." Once again, lay out any remaining index cards on a table before you. Scan them quickly, and select the cards of the offenders you have not yet forgiven because you do not fully understand their offenses against you. Make the decision to forgive each one even though you do not understand why they hurt you. Hold the cards in your hand while you pray the following prayer.

✪ **Prayer**

Father, I will never understand why people intentionally hurt and kill other people. You know that I have been hurt by [name your offender], and I do not understand why this person has hurt me. But, Lord, at this very moment, I choose to forgive. I know I may never in my lifetime understand why this person has hurt me in this horrible way. But, even so, my forgiveness for this person is complete, Lord. I can forgive because I know that you understand all things. And that I don't need to. I rest myself in your hands, Lord. In Jesus' name, amen.

Myth 4:

before forgiving the offender, you must feel forgiving and no longer be angry

> Do not conform any longer to the pattern of this world, but be transformed by the renewing of your mind. Then you will be able to test and approve what God's will is—his good, pleasing and perfect will.
>
> Romans 12:2

Has someone hurt you and you don't want to forgive because you don't feel forgiving? Most women who have been hurt harbor bitter emotions that interfere with the decision to forgive. Somehow, in spite of our hurt feelings, we must make a willful choice to forgive. God will help us with our feelings later in our forgiveness journey.

Joseph Polak knows about the price of unforgiveness. In 1945, when Joseph was only three years old, Nazi guards loaded him and his family into a freight car packed with 2,500 other people. They were moving the concentration camp survivors from Bergen-Belsen to another camp not far away. But the train engineer made a mistake. He missed his switch and, in the confusion, lost his way. For several days the engineer headed eastward. The prisoners were given no food or water. The train finally stopped at Troebetz. When the doors were opened, 500 people were dead. They had died horrible deaths. Many more people died soon afterward.

Joseph Polak survived the death train ride, but he could never forgive the Nazis for what they did. The feelings of hate ran too deep for too long.

Joseph grew up and became a rabbi in Boston—a city where I lived for many years. In 1995, in memory of those who had died, Polak and some of the other survivors planned a remembrance train ride that would take the same route the death train had taken from Belsen to Troebetz.

Before Polak and the other survivors boarded the train, officials of Belsen held a service for them. They wanted to give Polak an opportunity, after all the many years, to express his forgiveness to the train operator. But the bitterness in Polak's heart ran too deep. The pain hurt too much. He stood on the podium at Belsen and told the people he would not forgive them for the deeds of their parents. He told them they were doomed to be their representatives, that their hands would continue to be blood-stained.[10]

Because Joseph Polak didn't feel forgiving, he missed this rare opportunity to forgive.

Forgiveness is an act of the will. Know that you don't have to feel forgiving in order to forgive someone who hurts you. Neither must you rid yourself of feelings of anger.

"Sometimes people wonder how they could have forgiven someone when they are still angry at what she did. My response is: If you feel angry about what happened to you, congratulate yourself. Your anger is a clear sign that you are in touch with reality," writes Lewis Smedes.[11]

I feel angry when I hear about teenagers who kick to death a homeless man, or militant Hindus who burn missionaries alive, or murderers who shoot and kill their classmates. I feel angry when a friend's husband calls her names and belittles her in front of her friends, or when a child shouts obscenities to a loving parent, or when a neighbor gossips to other neighbors. Do you? Surely, our anger is justified, a natural human reaction.

According to Smedes, "If you weren't angry you would have lost one of the best parts of being human ... Anger is aimed at what persons do ... Anger keeps bad things from happening again to you ... Anger is the positive power that pushes us toward justice."[12]

The Reverend J. Robert Rioux knows about anger. He lost a long-time friend on September 11, 2001. His friend, Reverend Francis E. Grogan was aboard American Airlines Flight 175 when terrorists crashed the plane into the second World Trade Center tower. Rioux and Grogan had been friends since the 1940s. They attended seminary together. They had both retired to Holy Cross Father in Dartmouth, New Hampshire.

Going to visit his sister, Grogan bought a standby ticket direct from Boston to Los Angeles on September 11, 2001. That morning on television, Rioux and the other Holy Cross Fathers watched as Flight 175 crashed into the World Trade Center tower. They waited anxiously for a phone call from Father Grogan. They prayed that he had not found a standby seat on that flight. But the call never came. Father Grogan had been killed in that deliberate plane crash.

Father Rioux admits he agrees with Paul's words in Ephesians 4:31: "Get rid of all bitterness, rage and anger, brawling and slander, along with every form of malice." But he also admits, "There was anger at the injustice of it all, the fact he was torn away from us . . . your first impulse is, well, anger . . . Even priests have to work to get past their anger and move toward forgiveness. It's not always easy. We're still working on it today."

His anger, however, did not keep Rioux from forgiving the terrorists who killed his friend. Rioux spent much time in prayer and quiet reflection after his friend's death. He eventually chose to forgive.

"Forgiveness has to come somewhere down the line," Rioux confesses. "Eventually, you have to, or your own life will be ruined. You can't go through life with that anger."

Anger can be either harmful or helpful. Harmful anger shouts and screams and lashes out. Helpful anger, on the other hand, analyzes the tragedy. It hates the cruel offense but not the cruel offender. It forgives the offender and works hard to make sure the offense doesn't happen again. Helpful anger uses its energy to bring change and justice. Helpful anger rights wrongs. It can last a lifetime. Helpful anger can protect you, your family, and your community. It can keep you and others from suffering similar wounds in the future.

We can forgive an evildoer who has hurt us and still feel helpful anger over the senselessness and cruelty of the crime. But beware. Anger can be like fire. Though it can cook our food and keep us warm, it can also burn our flesh and destroy our home. Harmful anger can fill us with hate and resentment and bitterness, consume our health, and incinerate our relationships. Nothing good comes from harmful anger. Much good, however, comes from helpful anger—the act of forgiving the offender while hating the offense.

You can decide to travel the new direction toward pardon and release, no matter what your emotions summon. Once you decide to forgive, once you work your way through the forgiveness process, your "feelings of forgiveness" eventually will follow. One day as you look back on the painful incident, you may realize that the pain and anger in your heart has faded. When you remember the offender and the offense, you will no longer feel the hate and bitterness you once felt. And that's when you'll know that your forgiveness is complete.

Daily Sunlight

ℰ Interact with the Gardener

Read and reflect on Paul's advice to the Christians in Rome: "Do not conform any longer to the pattern of this world, but be transformed by the renewing of your mind. Then you will be able to test and approve what God's will is—his good, pleasing and perfect will" (Rom. 12:2).

In your opinion, how does a person conform to the pattern of this world? What is the pattern of this world? How can you and I be transformed by the renewing of our mind?

In your own words, write down God's good, pleasing, and perfect will concerning resentment and unforgiveness.

℮ Time to Grow

Now I want you to compare Joseph Polak's response to that of Pope John Paul II when he traveled to Athens, Greece, on May 4, 2001, to ask and receive forgiveness for sins committed by Roman Catholics against Orthodox Christians over the past 1,000 years. It was the first papal visit to Greece in 1,291 years!

"For the occasions past and present," stated the pope, "when sons and daughters of the Catholic Church have sinned by action or omission against their Orthodox brothers and sisters, may the Lord grant us forgiveness ... I am thinking of the disastrous sack of the imperial city of Constantinople [in 1204] which was for so long a bastion of Christianity in the East."

The pope also traveled to Damascus, Syria's capital. He addressed dozens of Syrian Christian and Islamic leaders, and sought their forgiveness. "For all the times that Muslims and Christians have offended one another," he said, "we need to seek forgiveness."

Then, on the spot where Saint Paul preached some 1,950 years ago, Pope John Paul met with Archbishop Christodoulos. The two men bowed their heads, and together prayed the Lord's Prayer: "Forgive us our trespasses as we forgive those who trespass against us."[13]

John Paul put aside 1,000 years of hurt feelings and, through forgiveness, made the first step in reconciliation. Healing can begin even after a millennium of bad feelings.

Now compare Joseph Polak's response of unforgiveness to that of Sevina Medina. In 1996, Valeria Eichmann traveled to Beth Sar Shalom, Argentina's first messianic synagogue, to ask forgiveness for the Holocaust atrocities committed against the Jewish people by her Nazi grandfather, Adolph Eichmann. At the end of her plea, Holocaust survivor Medina hugged Eichmann, as a symbol of accepting her apology on behalf of Jews.[14] We do not know if Medina felt forgiving at the time. We do, however, know that her forgiveness didn't change the evil of the Holocaust. Yet, her act of forgiveness contributed to much healing.

Did you list an offender on your index cards from whom you are withholding forgiveness because you don't feel forgiving or because you still feel angry? If so, pull the card from the remaining stack. Decide to forgive this person, and then pray the following prayer.

℮ **Prayer**

Lord, let me be truthful with you. I despise what [name your offender] did to me. I do not, in any way, feel forgiving toward this person. But I now see that my feelings have nothing to do with my decision, my will, to forgive. I choose to forgive, Lord, in spite of my feelings, in spite of my urge for retaliation. As of this moment, Father, I completely forgive [your offender]. I pray that you will enrich my heart with good feelings of forgiveness. I pray this prayer in Jesus' name, amen.

Myth 5: forgiving means the offender will face no consequences

One of the greatest barriers to forgiveness is the myth that forgiveness automatically frees our offender from any consequences for his actions. Such a misunderstanding makes many people hesitant to forgive and condemns them to a lifetime of unnecessary bitterness.

Robert Jeffress

A re you afraid to forgive your offender because you fear that person will not face any consequences for hurting you? As you and I both know, consequences usually follow wrongdoings. A consequence is a natural or necessary result of an action. For example, a consequence can be seen when you remove a hammered nail from a smooth board. The nail is gone, but you still have the nail hole in the board.

When someone commits a crime against you, you can choose to forgive. But, you can also be assured that your forgiveness will not erase the consequences of the offender's crime. The offender may still face arrest and punishment. Forgiveness doesn't mean that justice shouldn't be served. Even if the offender escapes imprisonment, the person must still live with the crime and the guilt it produces. The Bible also tells us that God will ultimately judge the offender (see Acts 17:31; Rom. 2:16; 2 Tim. 4:1; James 4:12; Rev. 20:12).

Do you remember the Old Testament story of David, the second king of Israel? Most Christians know David's story well. David was a warrior under King Saul. When he eventually became king, he committed a crime against a woman and her husband. He saw the beautiful Bathsheba as she bathed on her rooftop and he wanted her. He didn't care that Bathsheba was married to Uriah, one of his finest soldiers, who, at that very hour, was out fighting David's battles. He took Bathsheba to his bed and impregnated her. When David learned of Bathsheba's pregnancy, he reassigned Uriah to the front lines of the battlefield with the assumption he would be killed. After Uriah's death, David married Bathsheba and she bore him a son.

David thought he had covered his crimes well. But along came God's prophet Nathan, who pointed his finger in David's face and rebuked him for his sins. David was convicted of his sin, but Nathan responded: "The Lord has taken away your sin. You are not going to die [but] . . . the son born to you will die" (2 Sam. 12:13–14).

David asked God for mercy and God forgave David. God cleansed him from his sin because God is loving and compassionate. But David still had to face the consequences of his wrongdoings. The baby became ill. David pleaded with God to let the child live. David fasted and lay on the ground, refusing to get up or to eat. After seven days, the baby died, just as Nathan had predicted.

David paid a high price for his adultery with Bathsheba. God forgave David, but he still suffered the consequences of his act.

"We cannot undo our old mistakes or their consequences any more than we can erase old wounds that we have both suffered and inflicted," writes Frederick Buechner in his book *Telling Secrets*.[15]

Early one January morning in 1984, Pope John Paul visited a prisoner, Mehmet ali Agca, at the Rebibbia prison in Rome. A few weeks earlier, hidden in the shadowy nooks of the Vatican, Agca aimed a pistol at the pope and shot him in the chest. Fortunately John Paul recovered. On that January morning, the pontiff looked Agca in the eye, extended his hand, and said, "I forgive you."

Even though the pope forgave him, Agca still faced the consequences of his crime. "After Pope John Paul forgave a man who took a shot at him, a journalist commented: 'One forgives in one's heart, in the sight of God, as the pope did, but the criminal still serves his time in Caesar's jail.'"[16]

Sometimes victims will forgo forgiving because they want to make their offenders feel the pain they feel. However, no amount of unforgiveness can make an offender suffer your pain. Keeping alive the fires of hatred, resentment, and bitterness, will not cause the flames to burn your offenders. It just doesn't work that way. According to Chuck Colson, "Resentments are like eating rat poison and expecting the rat to get sick."

"If I forgive my coworker for stealing my idea and taking credit for it," a woman named Merry once told me, "I'll let her off the hook for what she did. I don't want to do that. I want her to suffer like I am suffering."

Pain and grief kept Merry so emotionally distraught, she no longer thought rationally. No amount of pain Merry suffers can make her betraying unrepentant coworker suffer. Her coworker may never feel a twinge of guilt or pain for stealing Merry's idea. When you choose to forgive someone, whether over a relational offense or a legal infraction, you forgive for your own good. You are the one who will benefit from your forgiveness, not your unrepentant offender.

Daily Sunlight

℮ Interact with the Gardener

The myth we studied today keeps many Christians from forgiving their offenders.

Read Psalm 32, and notice how David suffered from the unforgiven sins in his life. Think about how he describes the pain he experienced before he asked God for forgiveness.

Read Psalm 51. This is David's prayer of confession to God after his sin of adultery. What do you learn as you read David's agonizing prayer? What do you learn about God's complete forgiveness?

Read 1 Samuel 13:14. Why do you think God called David "a man after his own heart"?

Read 2 Samuel 12:24. How did God later comfort David's wife Bathsheba?

℮ Time to Grow

In *The Choosing to Forgive Workbook,* Les Carter and Frank Minirth write: "You cannot force another person to be aware of your feelings. You cannot make an individual accept responsibility for wrongdoing."[17] Why is this statement true?

How is resentment "like eating rat poison and expecting the rat to get sick"?

Why do you think most victims withhold forgiveness?

How does our forgiveness or unforgiveness have little to do with the offender's feelings? How can our unforgiveness make an offender suffer? Why is this not possible?

Lay out on a table all the offenders' cards you are still working toward forgiving. Ask yourself if today's myth is keeping you from forgiving any of them. Are you willing to allow God to be the judge of these offenders' crimes against you? Are you willing, right now, to release them from their debts—to completely forgive them—and let God face them with his consequences? If so, I want you to pull out those particular cards, hold each card in your hand one at a time, and pray this prayer.

@ **Prayer**

Father, I hold in my hands a card that represents an offender I have, at this very moment, decided to forgive. Lord, I completely forgive [name your offender]. I will trust you, Father, to judge this offender. I will trust you to order consequences in a way that will help each offender to see the crime and to learn a lesson from it. I am content now, Lord, to not wish cruel consequences on my offender, but to entrust you to deal with my offender as you see best. And, Father, even if my offender suffers no consequences in this life for unkind actions toward me, I'm okay with that too. Thank you for leading me to forgive. I promise to pray for [name your offender] as you bring that person's name to my mind. In Jesus' name, I thank you for the freedom that this forgiveness will bring. Amen.

◊ **A Light Sprinkling**

This week we examined five myths. Review these myths (below). Write down any additional thoughts that come to mind.

Myth 1: Forgiving means the offender didn't really hurt you

Myth 2: Forgiving means you condone or excuse the offender's hurtful act

Myth 3: Before forgiving, you must first understand why the offender hurt you

Myth 4: Before forgiving the offender, you must feel forgiving and no longer be angry

Myth 5: Forgiving means the offender will face no consequences

◊ **A Good Long Soaking**

1. Examine some of the following statements we studied this week.
    Do you agree or disagree with them, and why?

    a. "Forgiveness is not denying the reality of evil; in fact, forgive-
        ness begins by recognizing evil in all of its horror."[18]

        I agree with this statement because:

        I disagree with this statement because:

    b. "Forgiveness is a redemptive response to having been
        wronged and wounded ... Only those who have wronged and
        wounded us are candidates for forgiveness. If they injure us
        accidentally, we excuse them. We only forgive the ones we
        blame."[19]

        I agree with this statement because:

        I disagree with this statement because:

    c. "Our human minds yearn to understand why some people
        cause other people pain. We want to make all the confusing
        puzzle pieces fit before we can forgive and put the tragedy
        behind us."

        I agree with this statement because:

        I disagree with this statement because:

d. Our anger is justified, a natural human reaction. "If you weren't angry you would have lost one of the best parts of being human ... Anger is aimed at what persons do ... Anger keeps bad things from happening again to you ... Anger is the positive power that pushes us toward justice."[20]

I agree with this statement because:

I disagree with this statement because:

e. "Anger can be either harmful or helpful. Harmful anger shouts and screams and lashes out. Helpful anger, on the other hand, analyzes the tragedy. It hates the cruel offense, but not the cruel offender. It forgives the offender, and works hard to make sure the offense doesn't happen again. Helpful anger uses its energy to bring change and justice. Helpful anger rights wrongs. It can last a lifetime. Helpful anger can protect you, your family, and your community. It can keep you and others from suffering similar wounds in the future."

I agree with this statement because:

I disagree with this statement because:

2. Tell in your own words what you believe God's Word says about anger. Describe the difference between "helpful anger" and "harmful anger."

3. Delve into God's Word and see how Jesus used his "helpful anger" in good ways. Read Matthew 21:12–17 and reflect on Jesus' actions.

What triggered Jesus' helpful anger?

What did he do?

What did he say?

What was the result?

4. Describe how Father Rioux dealt with the loss of his friend.

5. Describe how anger can be like fire.

6. Robert Jeffress said, "One of the greatest barriers to forgiveness is the myth that forgiveness automatically frees our offender from any consequences for his actions. Such a misunderstanding makes many people hesitant to forgive and condemns them to a lifetime of unnecessary bitterness."[21]

   I agree with this statement because:

   I disagree with this statement because:

7. "We cannot undo our old mistakes or their consequences any more than we can erase old wounds that we have both suffered and inflicted."[22]

   I agree with this statement because:

   I disagree with this statement because:

◊ Weekend Feeding

Father, give me the courage of Missy Jenkins when she forgave the classmate that shot her and left her in a wheelchair. Give me the endurance of Gladys Staines who forgave those terrorists who murdered her husband and children and yet still chose to continue her missionary work in India. Help me to be like the Reverend J. Robert Rioux, who acknowledges his anger yet also understands that even priests have to work to get past their anger and move toward forgiveness. Show me the difference, Lord, between helpful anger and harmful anger. Help me, Father, to be less like the unforgiving Joseph Polak, and more like the forgiving Pope John Paul II and Savina Medina. Show me how to forgive those people who don't deserve forgiveness for their offenses. I pray all these things in Jesus' name, amen.

Myth 6:
forgiving means the offender must acknowledge and confess the offense, apologize, and seek forgiveness

> Does the victim depend on the culprit's contrition and confession as the precondition for being able to forgive? . . . If the victim could forgive only when the culprit confessed, then the victim would be locked into the culprit's whim, locked into victimhood, whatever her own attitude or intention.
>
> Desmond Tutu

Have you ever withheld forgiveness because your offender didn't acknowledge or confess the crime against you? We can lock ourselves into victimhood by refusing to forgive an offender until the crime is confessed. We might stay forever self-imprisoned.

In 1980, nineteen-year-old Catherine Gayle and a male friend picnicked on a pear farm near Sacramento, California. While they ate and laughed and enjoyed the sunny afternoon, a stranger, Douglas Mickey, sprung out of the woods and brutally stabbed them both to death. Mickey was arrested and received the death penalty for the murders. Catherine's mother, Aba Gayle, so hated Douglas Mickey for killing her daughter, she asked if she could watch Mickey's execution. Filled with anger and hate, she wanted to see him painfully pay for causing Catherine's death.

But Gayle found she couldn't live with her hate and her feelings for revenge. She sat down one night in 1992 and wrote Mickey a letter. She told him she had decided to forgive him. She told him she would even be willing to visit him in prison.

"The instant the letter was in the mailbox," Gayle remembers, "all the anger, all the rage, all the lust for revenge disappeared."

Forgiveness on Gayle's part was genuine and complete whether or not Mickey ever admitted to the murders.

Aba Gayle, however, had a surprise. Mickey read her letter and then wrote back. He acknowledged his crime—"an unspeakable burden to his soul," he called it. He said he would gladly give his own life if he could undo his violent crime.

Touched by his confession, Gayle decided to visit Mickey in prison. Since then, she has visited him several times. She now opposes the death penalty for Mickey and corresponds with him regularly, ministering to him by mail.[1]

Douglas Mickey acknowledged killing Aba Gayle's daughter, Catherine. He confessed his guilt. He yearned to undo the destruction he had caused. Gayle had forgiven him, however, long before his acknowledgment. Her forgiveness didn't rest on his confession. Neither did Aba Gayle's forgiveness depend upon his apology.

As Lewis Smedes writes, "The first and sometimes only person to get the benefits of forgiving is the person who does the forgiving."[2] Rare is the offender who apologizes and seeks your forgiveness. The words "I'm sorry" may thrill your heart when you hear them, but they are not needed for forgiveness to take place.

I often meet women who, as young children or teenagers, were sexually abused many years ago by a father or grandfather, older brother or uncle. You'd be shocked to learn just how many women in your family, church, or community have been sexually abused as little girls. Maybe you are a victim of childhood sexual molestation. Like most sexually abused women, perhaps you still harbor tremendous feelings of anger and bitterness toward your abuser. It is a natural human response. A sexual offender hurts us deeply. Like a dark lurking shadow, childhood sexual abuse may have followed you for a lifetime. It is likely the sexual offender never apologized to you. He might have denied it ever happened, moved away, disappeared, or died by the time you could finally face the fact of his abuse. You may yearn to meet with your offender, hear an apology from him, and then verbally forgive him. But that may no longer be possible.

What can you do? As an act of your will, you can take the first step and willingly choose to forgive. Whether he is alive or dead, whether he denies it or confesses it, whether the words "I'm sorry" ever leave his lips, you can still forgive him. One-sided forgiveness is genuine forgiveness whether or not your offender is present or involved. With God's help, through the process of forgiveness—even one-sided forgiveness—you can release the pain and shame you have suffered a lifetime. You can refuse to be further victimized by the hurtful memories. You can forgive him and move forward in your life.

In his book *Telling Secrets,* Frederick Buechner writes about his father's death on a November morning in 1936. Frederick was ten years old when his father got up early, put on slacks and a sweater, and peeked into his room. Then he went into the closed garage, started up the family Chevy, and breathed in the car's exhaust until it killed him. He never apologized for leaving Frederick fatherless.

Frederick's dad was cremated, and the family held no funeral. Frederick's mother gathered up her young sons and moved them far away to Bermuda. The family never spoke about his father again.

For decades, Frederick lived with secret grief and anger and guilt over his father's suicide. He could find no healing from his resentment and bitterness until he decided to forgive him. Forgiveness proved to be a lifelong journey. Eventually Buechner decided to forgive his father—with or without an apology.[3]

Does such forgiveness mean reconciliation or reunion? We will discuss that. But one-sided forgiveness on your part can be complete even when there is no repentance, no remorse. The choice and potential freedom is in your control, not in the control of your offender.

Daily Sunlight

@ Interact with the Gardener

In today's Bible study, we'll read Romans 12:17, 19. After you read Paul's words, answer the following three questions:

- What does Paul say about repaying evil for evil? (v. 17)
- What does Paul tell us about revenge? (v. 19)
- What does Paul mean when he writes: "It is mine to avenge; I will repay," says the Lord"?

According to Paul, how must you and I respond to evil people? (Rom. 12:19–20)

How did Aba Gayle live out this biblical principle?

How did Aba's action affect Mickey?

Reflect on Desmond Tutu's statement: "If the victim could forgive only when the culprit confessed, then the victim would be locked into the culprit's whim, locked into victimhood, whatever her own attitude or intention."[4] As you think about your own offenders, list the people who have not acknowledged or confessed their hurt to you. Has their lack of acknowledgement or confession kept you from forgiving them?

@ Time to Grow

From your stack of index cards, choose the offenders who have never apologized for hurting you. Ask yourself this question: Am I failing to forgive this person because I have not received an apology?

Turn to Acts 6:8–8:1 and reread the story of Stephen's stoning and death. Notice that Stephen forgave his murderers (7:59–60) even though they never apologized nor asked his forgiveness.

Now turn to Luke 23:32–38 and reread Jesus' crucifixion. Notice that Jesus forgave his murderers (v. 34) even though they never apologized nor asked his forgiveness.

Think about this: Those who stoned Stephen, as well as those who crucified Jesus, thought they were obeying Moses' Law (see Lev. 24:10–16). In that day, Jews who blasphemed against God were put to death. The Jews thought both Stephen and Jesus were guilty of blasphemy. They didn't apologize because they thought they had done nothing that needed their apology.

Consider this possibility: Could your offenders have failed to apologize to you because they thought they had done nothing that needed their apology? (Your answer may very well be no, but this thought needs to be considered.)

℮ **Prayer**

Father, I know I am not forgiving my offenders because they have not acknowledged their crimes nor have they confessed them. I must admit, Lord, that I have always thought that my forgiveness rested on an acknowledgment or confession from them. Today, however, I see how that myth has kept me "locked into the culprit's whim." That myth has "locked me into victimhood." I pray that I can be free, Father, from my self-made prison. At this very moment, Lord, I want to forgive [name your offenders] for their crimes against me. Even though they have not acknowledged or confessed the ways they have hurt me, I choose to forgive them. Please give me the unexplainable heart-peace that only forgiveness can bring. In Jesus' name I pray, amen.

Myth 7:
before you forgive, the offender must compensate you and restore your loss

> Forgiveness is not a *quid pro quo* deal—it doesn't demand compensation first. Forgiveness is one person's moral response to another's injustice.
>
> International Forgiveness Institute

Compensation means to pay back, to reimburse someone for a loss. Restitution is similar to compensation. Restitution is the act of giving something back to its rightful owner, or giving the equivalent of something that has been lost or damaged. Restoration means to give something back that was lost, to make it look like it originally looked. After Jesus forgave him, traitor-tax collector Zacchaeus sought to restore the money he had stolen from his own people. As a chief tax collector working for the Romans, Zacchaeus became wealthy at the expense of the Jews he exploited. His unjust actions alienated him from family, friends, and society. In those days, the people you invited to sit around your dinner table indicated your social status in the community. No one dared invite Zacchaeus to eat with him for good reason. He was an outcast. He would tarnish their reputation.

When he climbed a sycamore-fig tree to watch Jesus pass by, Jesus stopped, looked up into the tree, and invited Zacchaeus to dinner. So grateful to be accepted by Jesus, Zacchaeus exclaimed, "Look, Lord! Here and now I give half of my possessions to the poor, and if I have cheated anybody out of anything, I will pay back four times the amount"

(Luke 19:8). Zacchaeus found acceptance and forgiveness. In turn, he wanted to reimburse, to repay, to refund, to restore all the money he had selfishly pocketed.

But offenders can take from us precious things that can never be given back. Desmond Tutu, the retired archbishop of Cape Town, South Africa, knows about the loss of precious things that cannot be compensated or restored. For most of his lifetime, Tutu struggled against apartheid in South Africa. Not until April 27, 1994, was Tutu finally given the opportunity to vote in a democratic election in the town of his birth. During apartheid, Tutu remembers the people who were teargassed, bitten by police dogs, struck with batons, detained, tortured, banned, imprisoned, sentenced to death, and sent into exile. He recalls the violent abuse black South Africans suffered from the hands of white landowners. Apartheid provided the whites with enormous privileges, leaving its black victims deprived and exploited. During apartheid, gross human violations against black South Africans became a way of life.

Black South Africans, while given the right to vote, will never be compensated for their enormous losses. Desmond Tutu knows that, yet he has spent his life trying to right the wrong of apartheid. He has preached the message of forgiveness, that for Christians "the death and resurrection of Jesus Christ is proof positive that love is stronger than hate, that life is stronger than death, that light is stronger than darkness, that laughter and joy, and compassion and gentleness and truth, all these are so much stronger than their ghastly counterparts."[5] He has urged black South Africans to forgive their longtime abusers, for he has witnessed the vicious effects of unforgiveness.

"Our unforgiveness undoes us," Tutu writes. "Anger, hatred, resentment, bitterness, revenge—they are death-dealing spirits, and they will 'take our lives' on some levels ... I believe the only way we can be whole, healthy, happy persons is to learn to forgive."[6]

Desmond Tutu is right when he writes: "It isn't easy, as we all know ... to forgive, but we are people who know that when someone cannot be forgiven there is no future."[7]

Daily Sunlight

@ Interact with the Gardener

From your cards, select those offenders you haven't yet forgiven because they haven't yet compensated you for the hurts they caused you. Hold them in your hands while you work through today's Bible study.

Read the story of Zacchaeus in Luke 19:1–10. Imagine the scene as described by Luke. Envision the city of Jericho, the short man Zacchaeus, the crowd of people, the sycamore-fig tree, and Zacchaeus's proclamation after Jesus invites him to a meal.

When Zacchaeus climbed down from the tree, what was his promise to Jesus?

Why did Jesus' supper invitation surprise Zacchaeus?

In Jesus' day, how did Jewish people feel about tax collectors?

@ Time to Grow

How would you describe the difference between compensation and restitution?

What are the things in life that can never be repaid or restored? Have any of these offenders (listed on the index cards you hold in your hand) ever hurt you in a way that cannot be compensated? How?

Will you decide right now to forgive these offenders even though they will probably never compensate you for your pain and loss?

℆ **Prayer**

Father, I absolutely hate what [name your offender] has done to me and/or to those people I love. This offender could never begin to compensate me, or my family, for what they've taken away. Until now, Lord, I believed I could not forgive this offender unless I was compensated first. I know now, Lord, that this is just a myth—a dangerous myth that has kept me from forgiving. I have decided, Lord, at this very moment, as an act of my will, that I will forgive [name your offender]. In spite of what that person took from me, I choose to forgive. Even though I will never regain my loss, I still choose to forgive. Please bring me the peace that only this type of forgiveness will bring. I pray all these things in the name of your son, amen.

Myth 8:
when your offender is punished, you'll find healing and closure

Bear with each other and forgive whatever grievances you may have against one another. Forgive as the Lord forgave you.

Colossians 3:13

I hope you have never and will never experience a loved one's murder. I have met many people, throughout my lifetime, who have grieved for decades over a husband or parent or child or sibling who has been murdered. They each have had to work through the tough process of total forgiveness. The ones who have chosen to forgive the murderer have experienced a rare peace in their souls. The ones who haven't chosen to forgive, however, are still daily tortured by the heinous crime of the offender.

I tell you the following story to show that even execution (of a child's murderer) will not bring you healing or closure. Only forgiveness promises to bring you emotional recovery and conclusion. After the execution of murderer Dennis Dowthitt, grieving mother Linda Purnhagen found no satisfying end to her suffering or bitterness.

On June 13, 1990, Linda saw her two daughters, sixteen-year-old Gracie and nine-year-old Tiffany, for the last time. Delton Dowthitt, a school friend of both girls, and his father, Dennis, a dangerously sick psychopath, picked up the girls from a bowling alley and drove to a deserted place. Dennis Dowthitt strangled Tiffany to death, raped Gracie, and slit her throat.

When authorities discovered the girls' bodies, they arrested and convicted Dennis and scheduled his October 7, 1992, execution. During the trial, Dowthitt's own daughters, Donna and Darla, testified that their father had threatened them with a knife and raped them as teenagers.[8]

A decade later, as executioners strapped him to his death-gurney, Dennis Dowthitt apologized for the savage killings. "I am so sorry for what y'all had to go through," he sobbed, choking on his words. "You had some lovely girls and I am sorry."

It was the first time Linda Purnhagen heard Dowthitt admit to the murders. But not even Dowthitt's confession, apology, and execution brought healing and closure for Linda. She watched the executioner pump the deadly drugs through needles into Dowthitt's body. She saw his body quiver and then fall limp. But she was disappointed after the execution, not relieved. She was still hurting, not healed. In her heart, she had a huge gaping cavity.

"My daughters went through horrible deaths," Purnhagen said. "[Dowthitt] just went to sleep. [His execution] doesn't make me feel any better."[9]

Bill Chadwick experienced the same lack of closure. On October 23, 1993, his son, Michael, was killed by a speeding drunk driver. The drunk driver was arrested and served six months in boot camp. But Bill, like Linda Purnhagen, also discovered that arrest and justice do not bring healing and closure. Bill admits he felt angry.

"I guess I had bought into the belief that, somehow, things would be different after the driver had been brought to justice. I think that is what people mean when they talk about 'getting closure.' We think that if there is someone to blame, then we can put the matter to rest."

But Bill couldn't put the matter to rest. Months passed with no relief from his pain and anger. Then Bill Chadwick made the decision to forgive the drunk driver who had killed his son. Even though the road to forgiveness was long and painful, Bill made a wonderful discovery. "Until I could forgive the driver," he claims, "I would not get the closure I was looking for. Forgiving is different from removing responsibility. The driver was still responsible for Michael's death, but I had to forgive him before I could let the incident go. No amount of punishment could ever even the score."[10]

If you are putting off forgiving your offenders because you hope justice, imprisonment, or execution will bring you needed healing, please rethink your decision. Only your complete forgiveness for the wicked offender will put an end to your pain.

Daily Sunlight

@ Interact with the Gardener

Read Colossians 3:13 and reflect on its meaning while you answer the following questions:

How did Linda Purnhagen finally find closure after the murder of her two young daughters?

How did Bill Chadwick finally find closure after a drunk driver killed his son, Michael?

What do these two stories have in common with Colossians 3:13? What do they tell you about forgiving others who seriously hurt you or the people you love?

@ Time to Grow

Now, find at least three different Bible translations. In each translation, look up the verse in Colossians 3:13 and read it aloud. Choose your favorite translation of this verse, and read it again—slowly, concentrating on each individual word. Write the verse and insert the names of your offenders (listed on the cards).

Paul writes: "Bear with _____, and forgive whatever grievances you may have against one another. Forgive _____ as the Lord forgave you" (Col. 3:13).

What advice do you hear Paul speaking directly to you in this verse?

Are you willing to forgive _____ for offenses against you?

Before you pray, take a moment to read aloud their names and your comments penned on each card.

@ **Prayer**

Father, today I have learned that closure, healing, and peace come only through forgiving those offenders who have hurt me. Lord, right now, at this very moment, I want to forgive [name your offender]. I release this person, Lord, from wicked offenses. Please replace the horrible hurt in my heart with your generous peace. I pray that you will keep me from ever dwelling on these offenders or their crimes. Give me the peace you promise in your Word—peace beyond my understanding. Thank you, Jesus, for the sweet peace of your forgiveness. In Jesus' name, amen.

Myth 9:
forgiving means the offender won't hurt you again, and that you must reconcile and reunite

One of the most basic hindrances to forgiveness is the fear of further abuse. We have a legitimate concern that forgiving our offender will give him permission to hurt us even more deeply.

Robert Jeffress

A re you afraid to forgive someone because, if you do, that person might hurt you again?

Late one night, I received a phone call from a woman I didn't know. I'll call her Janice. She had heard me speak on spousal abuse and wanted to ask me some questions. Married to a prominent bank president, she had forgiven her husband time and time again for his physical and emotional abuse. But, as in most spousal abuse cases, his battering had intensified. She told me he had just knocked out her front teeth. She was desperate. She wanted to forgive him, but she didn't want to give him permission to hit her again.

"Every time I forgive him," she cried, "I become a doormat for him to step on again. It has happened over and over. I don't know what to do. I can't go through another battering episode like tonight!"

"Janice," I told her. "I'm glad you called me."

I gave her the name of a local women's shelter and urged her to pack a few clothes and go there immediately. I also gave her the name and number of a wonderful Christian counselor in the city. I knew him well and knew he could help her.

Janice took my advice and got the help she needed.

I am always amazed at the great number of battered Christian women I meet in my travels across the United States and around the world. They meet with me after I speak, and they whisper in my ear their secret pain. Did you know that, just in the United States, approximately four million women are abused by current or former spouses every year?[11] Abused women sit beside you and me in church pews on Sundays. They go to our Sunday school classes and community Bible studies. They live in fear of the next battering episode. They often talk with their church pastors about the abuse. And, surprisingly, the advice they are often given sends them back into the violent home, putting their lives in danger.

A recent survey asked 5,700 pastors how they would counsel a woman who was the target of spousal abuse. Their answers shocked me. No doubt, they will shock you too.

- 26% would counsel a woman to continue to submit [to her husband]
- 25% said the wife's failure to submit was the cause of the abuse in the first place
- 50% said women should tolerate some level of violence in the home because it is better than divorce
- 71% said they would never counsel a battered wife to leave her husband
- 92% said they would never suggest divorce

Those who conducted the survey noted that "today's pastor/church leadership seem unable to help hurting women, especially in cases of domestic violence."[12]

This type of "counseling" could put a battered woman and her children in extreme danger.

Perhaps you have been the victim of spousal abuse. If so, know that abuse cannot be tolerated. You don't have to take that kind of harsh treatment! Know that you can forgive your abusive husband, and, at the same time, refuse to stay under the same roof with him. Your forgiveness does not give your spouse permission to hurt you or your children.

Until your abusive spouse receives treatment and is cured from this battering sickness, reunion should not take place. It's too dangerous.

I am so pleased to read what the Reverend Frank A. Thomas writes:

> I do not believe that it is God's will for any person to stay in a violent and abusive relationship under the justification that God does not condone divorce. I am not advocating divorce, or an easy exit from the lifelong commitment of marriage, but I believe that God does not desire that anyone subject themselves to abuse and violence. I do not believe that God requires any spouse to be beaten as a part of the marriage covenant. Therefore, if someone is abusive, then the victim of the crime by all means has the right to leave.[13]

You may think of spousal abuse only as *physical* ill treatment. But abuse can also be *emotional.* Women tell me that name-calling, harsh criticism, foul damaging language, and other emotionally abusive acts hurt even more than physical violence. With emotional abuse, women suffer bruises on the inside. They tell me that can hurt even more than bruises on their arms and legs.

"Cruelty is generally thought of in terms of physical pain," writes Karl Menninger. "But there is a kind of personal injury, given and taken, which is not physically but psychologically painful, and which may also be . . . damaging. I refer to the use of words as weapons."[14]

We have seen from his Word that God does, however, want us to forgive those who hurt us—even an abusive spouse. But that certainly does not mean that you must lower your personal safety boundaries. Forgiving an abusive husband is for your sake, not for his sake.

Forgiving your abuser and not allowing him to hurt you further also applies to abusive parents, siblings, family members, grown children, coworkers, neighbors, and so on. You can forgive an abuser and, at the same time, protect yourself from further abuse. Your forgiveness never gives another person the right to hurt you again.

As Smedes explains, "Forgiving a person does not mean that we tolerate what that person is doing to hurt us. Forgiving does not turn us into mush."[15]

Forgiving an offender doesn't mean you must reconcile and reunite either. Paul Meier writes: "Forgiving a jerk who abuses you doesn't mean that you have to cozy up to that jerk and become fast friends. In fact, in most cases, you will need to keep away from jerks who abuse you. Avoid them, if possible. If necessary, change jobs, golf partners, or the route you drive to work."[16]

Are you afraid to forgive someone who has hurt you because you think forgiveness always means reconciliation and reunion with the offender and getting together with that person is the last thing you ever want to do?

Reconciliation means bringing hearts and minds together again. It takes two people to reconcile. Confession, repentance, apology, and acceptance are all needed for reconciliation to take place. We can choose to forgive someone who hurts us and, at the same time, choose *not* to reconcile. Forgiveness is genuine even when it does not include reconciliation. Much will depend, of course, on your relationship before the hurtful offense, as well as the offense itself.

While forgiveness takes only one person to accomplish it, reconciliation takes two. While reconciliation presents the ideal situation after forgiveness takes place, it's just not always possible or preferable. Some reconciliation will never take place in this life.

Reunion is the decision to come together again after a period of separation. It does not, however, give the offender permission to inflict more pain.

You can seek reconciliation without reuniting. Some relationships, however, should strive for reconciliation and reunion, if at all possible. Parents and children, siblings, husbands and wives, in-laws and family members, church members, coworkers, neighbors, and so forth, have bonds that mean more than those of casual acquaintances or strangers. Marriage fits especially well into this category.

"Without forgiveness, sin will destroy a marriage," admits author Walter Wangerin. "Forgiveness is daily renewal. It's like your blood—it keeps pumping through your body, picking up fresh oxygen and renewing every cell. If that renewal stops, death begins. Forgiveness is a marriage's lifeblood."[17]

In the case of an abusive marriage, however, separation must happen for the sake of safety. The couple should forgive and work toward reconciliation and reunion, but not until the battering spouse gets treatment and the home situation becomes safe.

"If you're married to a jerk, get counseling. If the abuse by a jerky partner gets too severe, separate until your mate gets counseling and the situation is safe. Moving out of masochism into maturity does not mean becoming a doormat. In fact, that's what a masochist is—a doormat who has probably been stuffing his or her anger and trying to believe that this is the way to be 'spiritual.'"[18]

While, in many cases, reconciliation and reunion are the hoped-for ideals of forgiveness, forgiving an offender does not depend on them.

Daily Sunlight

@ Interact with the Gardener

Read 1 Peter 3:1–7. Define the word *submissive*. Also read Ephesians 5:21–33. How does God intend a husband and wife to relate to each other?

How can the word *submit* unwisely send a wife back to an abusive husband? What advice would you give to an abused wife?

Read Romans 12:18. What advice does Paul give and why?

Why do you think Paul prefaces his words with: "if it is possible" and "as far as it depends on you"?

@ Time to Grow

Why do you believe many pastors recommend women to return to an abusive husband? Did the statistics, and their answers, surprise you? Why? Have you ever been given that advice by a pastor or Christian counselor?

Why is this following statement true? "Forgiving a person does not mean that we tolerate what that person is doing to hurt us. Forgiving does not turn us into mush." Do you think that forgiving your offender will turn you into "mush"? Do you have friends who believe this? What would you wish to tell them? What have you told them in the past?

Robert Jeffress writes: "One of the most basic hindrances to forgiveness is the fear of further abuse. We have a legitimate concern that forgiving our offender will give him permission to hurt us even more deeply."[19] Do you have someone in your life that is abusive? If you do, you have probably already written the offender's name on one of your index cards. Find that card(s). Hold it in your hand while you pray. Decide once and for all that you will forgive this offender, but that you will not allow them to hurt you again.

℮ **Prayer**

Father, [name your offender] is abusing or hurting me. I want to follow your Word, Lord, and forgive my offender for "whatever grievances" that person has caused me. But, if I do, Lord, I don't want to think I am giving them permission to hurt me again. Give me the grace and strength to forgive [your offender]. I want to forgive at this very moment. I can see now, Lord, after studying your Word, it is a myth to believe that "forgiving means the offender won't hurt me again." Protect me, Father. Give me divine wisdom. I will depend upon your wisdom, Lord, and your Word for my guidance.

Before I close this prayer, Lord, may I also pray for all those women in the world who live with abuse—especially spousal abuse. I've read the statistics, Lord. I know they are legion. Please give them the strength to forgive, and also the courage to leave the abusers until their abusers receive treatment for their abusing sickness. In Jesus' name, amen.

Myth 10: some crimes are too horrible to forgive

I'm going to have to come up with a new word. Indifferent isn't enough. Cruel isn't enough to say. Heartless? Inhumane? Maybe we've just redefined inhumanity here.

Richard Alpert

Some crimes seem far too horrible to forgive. They are heartless. Inhumane. We wonder if some acts of cruelty even deserve our forgiveness. The story of Chante Mallard and Gregory Biggs fits under this category.

Thirty-seven-year-old Gregory Biggs had fallen on hard times. A homeless man, he paid small amounts of money to sleep in a homeless shelter at night. His son, Brandon, a college student, visited him often. Together they shopped and talked and enjoyed a good relationship.

On October 26, 2001, a car driven by a nurse's aide, Chante Mallard, hit Gregory Biggs as he crossed the street. The impact broke his leg and thrust him head first into her windshield. Chante didn't stop but drove home—some eight miles—with Biggs lodged in her broken windshield. Ignoring Biggs's pleas for help, she parked her car in the garage and left him stuck in her windshield for three days.

When Biggs finally bled to death from his wounds, Chante and a friend dumped his body in the trunk of her car and drove away. Police found the body discarded in a vacant park. Four months later, police arrested Chante.

Mallard blamed her cruel behavior on the alcohol and drugs she had used prior to the accident. Gregory's mother, Meredith, wondered how

Chante could leave her son to die like that since drugs and alcohol wear off. She wonders why Chante didn't get some help for him when she sobered up.

During the trial, Chante apologized to the Biggs family. The judge sentenced her to fifty years in prison. What happened after Chante's sentencing, however, proves that no crime is too horrible to forgive. When Biggs' college-aged son, Brandon, stepped up to the microphone, his words surprised everyone in the courtroom. He told the Mallard family that his family was also sorry for their loss as well. And to Chante, he told her he accepted her apology and hoped she would accept his forgiveness and the forgiveness of Jesus Christ.

Later, on Larry King Live, Brandon Biggs talked about his father, the murder, Chante Mallard, and the trial. "We would like to offer our forgiveness to Chante Mallard," he said.

A viewer called in and asked Brandon, "How could you possibly forgive Chante for killing your father?!"

Brandon said softly, "It comes because I've been forgiven for so much ... I can't not be forgiving. Life is too short to live with all the anger and bitterness ... life's too short for that."[20]

Has someone hurt you so deeply and horribly that you think you can't forgive? If so, please know that forgiveness is possible even for the most horrible crimes, the most inhumane offenders. I beg you to choose to forgive those who have hurt you, not just for the sake of the offender, but for your own sake. The offender might care nothing about your forgiveness or even receive your forgiveness. But forgiveness will begin your own healing. Even though the crime was brutal, unspeakable, degrading, and inhumane, don't let its horror keep you from finding your heart's peace through forgiveness.

Daily Sunlight

@ Interact with the Gardener

If you or a loved one have ever been the victim of crimes you thought too horrible to forgive, maybe the following exercise will help you to forgive your offenders. (I would suggest you do this exercise with the help of a Christian counselor.)

Close your eyes. Envision the offenders' faces. Then, in your imagination, stand face to face with the offenders. Stretch out your hand and extend it to them, one at a time. Imagine that you are conversing with your offenders. Tell the offenders how their crimes deeply wounded you. Tell them that their crimes are too horrible to forgive. Now tell them that, in spite of their horrible crimes, you have chosen to forgive them. All of them. Tell them your forgiveness is a gift to them—nothing they could ever earn, and certainly nothing they deserve. One at a time, grasp each offender's hand. Tell that person that you forgive the crimes committed against you.

Do you have any index cards of offenses "too horrible to forgive"? On each card, write the following message: "To: _____ (the offender's name). You do not deserve my forgiveness. The crime you committed against me was horrible, inhumane. But I have chosen to forgive you." Then sign your name at the bottom of the card.

@ Time to Grow

Let's take a few minutes to study God's Word.

Peter committed a horrible crime against Jesus when he denied him (see John 18:15–18). Describe the scene of Peter's harsh denial.

Read John 21:15–24. How did Jesus forgive and reinstate Peter? What did Jesus tell Peter to do? How did Peter accept his forgiveness? What did Jesus mean when he said, "Feed my lambs . . . Take care of my sheep"? Why did Jesus ask Peter the same question three times: "Simon son of John, do you truly love me?"

Jesus faced arrest, torture, and crucifixion—crimes we might consider "too horrible to forgive." Read the prayer Jesus prayed prior to his arrest (see John 17). What did Jesus ask for himself? For his disciples? For unborn believers? Did God answer his prayer? Why?

Did Brandon Biggs's response of forgiveness to Chante Mallard surprise you? In your opinion, why did he choose to forgive her for his father's cruel death? What would you have said to Chante had you been Brandon?

@ **Prayer**

Jesus, how could you have forgiven Peter when he purposely denied you? Surely, that was a horrible crime. How could you have forgiven the savages who nailed you to the cross? Show me, Lord, how to forgive those who might inflict horror and pain upon me and my loved ones. Help me to remember that no crime is too horrible to forgive. Forgiveness is possible even in the most heinous, inhumane crimes.

Father, I have just chosen to forgive [name your offender] even though the offense against me seems too horrible to forgive. I pray you will fill my heart and life with forgiveness, now and in the future. In Jesus' name I pray, amen.

Weekly Watering

◊ A Light Sprinkling

This week we examined five myths. Review these and respond to the questions or quotes beneath each one.

1. Forgiving means the offender must acknowledge and confess the offense, apologize, and seek forgiveness.

   Name three reasons why this statement is a myth.

2. Before you forgive, the offender must compensate you and restore your loss.

   Rape victim Debbie Morris writes: "There are times when forgiveness won't, and shouldn't, result in restoration. There are cases, like my experience with Robert Willie, where there never was a relationship to be restored, when the highest goal we should seek is salvage."[21] By "salvage," Debbie means "to find a way to get over the incident, to minimize the damage, to get on with the healing, to learn from the experience, and to move on. Making the best you can from a past experience is the goal of ... 'salvage.'"[22] Do you agree or disagree with Debbie's statement? Why?

3. When your offender is punished, you'll find healing and closure.

   Did grieving mother, Linda Purnhagen, find healing after murderer Dennis Dowthitt was executed? What is the only way to find healing and closure after an intentional offense?

4. Forgiving means the offender won't hurt you again, and that you must reconcile and reunite.

   a. Define *reconciliation*. Define *reunion*. Name the times in a woman's life when she should not reconcile or reunite with someone.

   b. Does genuine forgiveness depend on reconciliation and reunion? Why?

   c. What advice would you give to an abused wife or husband?

   d. Why do you believe some women think it is "not spiritual" to "move out of masochism into maturity"?

   e. Have you ever in your life felt like a doormat? What precipitated this feeling?

   f. Read this statement by Lewis Smedes and write down several comments that come to mind: "We can see the differences between forgiving and reunion clearly if we look at them both from several sides: It takes one person to forgive. It takes two to be reunited ... Forgiving happens inside the wounded person. Reunion happens in a relationship between people ... We can forgive a person who never says he is sorry. We cannot be truly reunited unless he is honestly sorry ... We can forgive even if we do not trust the person who wronged us once not to wrong us again. Reunion can happen only if we can trust the person who wronged us once not to wrong us again ... Forgiving has no strings attached. Reunion has several strings attached."[23]

5. Some crimes are too horrible to forgive.

Name those offenses you've heard or read about that you think are too horrible to forgive. Have you suffered a "too-horrible-to-forgive" offense in your own life? Describe it/them.

◊ A Good Long Soaking

1. Read Romans 12:18: What advice does Paul give and why?

2. Read aloud Psalm 23. Write down the images that bring you peace and comfort.

3. Arrange your index cards into two stacks. One stack will be all those offenders you have chosen to forgive so far, from Week One to this week. The other stack will be all those offenders you have yet to forgive. Place two chairs facing each other. While holding the stacks of cards of those offenders you've already chosen to forgive, sit down in one of the chairs. Choose one card at a time. Imagine this offender sits in the chair that faces you. Speaking aloud, call the person by name, and tell this offender exactly what you have forgiven and why you have forgiven. (Example: "Your name is _____. I have chosen to forgive you for your offenses against me. I am forgiving you for [list the offenses]. As of right now, you no longer owe me a debt. I have forgiven the debt you owe me. I have chosen to forgive you because [list the benefits forgiveness will bring you]. You are forgiven—completely and forever.") Tear the card into small pieces. Slowly let the pieces fall out of your hands and into a trash can. On a blank sheet of

paper, write down the forgiven offender's name. Beside the name write the word *forgiven.*

4. Let's talk for a moment about forgiving and forgetting. William A. Meninger writes, "At times we refuse to forgive because we think that this means we have to bury some past painful event or at least pretend that it never happened. Forgiveness is not forgetting. We remember the pain and will always bear the scar of a past hurt."[24]

When someone deliberately hurts you, can you ever forget the pain they caused? Must you always seek to forget when you seek to forgive? I hope your answer is no, because forgiving does not mean forgetting. Only in a brain-dead state could we forget the horrors inflicted on us by others. Some abuses we will remember for a lifetime. The pain might fade, but the scar stays forever. The same thing happens when we decide to forgive ourselves for an offense we commit. We can forgive ourselves completely and still remember our shortcomings. Remembering our failures will instill within us lessons only pain can teach us.

5. Read Hebrews 8:12 and Jeremiah 31:34. "But," you say, "doesn't the writer of Hebrews, speaking of the houses of Israel and Judah, quote Jeremiah when he writes, 'For I will forgive their wickedness and will *remember their sins no more*'"?

Indeed, he does. But is "remembering their sins no more" the same as "forgetting their sins"? Look up the word *forget* in a dictionary. Doesn't it mean "to lose (facts, knowledge, etc.) from the mind; to fail to recall; to be unable to remember"? Do you believe that Almighty God, Creator of heaven and earth, can "lose facts from his mind"? Can he "fail to recall"? Can he "be unable to remember"? Do you think a better definition in this case might be: "God chooses to hold the sin against us no longe?. He chooses to release us from the wrong, to restore us? When God looks at us, when he hears our prayers, he willingly chooses not to see the sin anymore—the sin he has decided to 'forgive and forget'"? Why or why not?

6. Read Philippians 3:13. What does it mean to "forget what is behind and strain toward what is ahead"? We can choose to forgive the person who hurt us, and to get on with our lives and work. We can decide not to hold the sin against him, to release him from his wrong, and, in some cases, to reconcile and reunite. But to forget the lessons pain teaches us would be a tragedy in itself. We need not dwell on them, nor further inflict our minds with the pain of their memory. But, to forget those hard-learned lessons—to permanently erase them from our mind—might lead us to repeat the pain, or have the pain repeated to us. We must remember suffering—not with resentment and hatred and bitterness—but with wisdom, so that it never happens again. Desmond Tutu agrees: "In forgiving, people are not being asked to forget. On the contrary, it is important to remember, so that we should not let such atrocities happen again."[25] Do you agree or disagree? Why?

◊ Weekend Feeding

Lord, thank you for helping me to forgive those offenders and their offenses that now lay in tiny pieces in the trash can. If they should ever come to my mind again, Father, I pray that my only response will be to pray for them.

As I continue working through this Bible study, I pray that you will continue to help me undertake my journey of forgiveness. I realize that if I am harboring unforgiveness toward anyone, I will find that my usefulness in your kingdom is sadly diminished. Help me to examine your Word, as well as society's myths about forgiveness, and to forgive all my offenders. Help me to forgive them, Lord, like you forgave those who crucified you. I pray these things in Jesus' name, amen.

experiencing the miracle
of *forgiveness*

Forgiving Others Frees Us to Flourish

The little girl in the newspaper

Finally, brothers, whatever is true, whatever is noble, whatever
is right, whatever is pure, whatever is lovely, whatever is
admirable—if anything is excellent or praiseworthy—think
about such things.

Philippians 4:8

Phan Thi Kim Phuc was the nine-year-old South Vietnamese girl who
covered the front pages of newspapers during the Vietnam War era.
A photographer took her photo as she ran naked down the street, her
flesh on fire. Jellied napalm seared her skin after a U.S. commander
ordered a bomb attack on her city. The photo shocked the world.

"The little girl's arms were stretched out as though in supplication, her
face contorted in a scream of pain and terror," writes Chuck Colson. The
painful image earned the photographer, Nick Ut of the Associated Press,
a Pulitzer Prize, and helped turn the heart of a nation against the war.

Ut rushed the girl to the hospital, and the doctors treated her for
severe third-degree burns. Napalm left her skin permanently scarred and
deeply ridged.

Phan Thi Kim Phuc survived. We would expect her to be filled with
bitter resentment and deep hatred in her heart for all Americans. She
wore on her skin the ugly scars of a confusing war. Each glance into a
mirror reminded her of the painful trauma. But Kim's life took a much
different turn from the expected.

At an impressionable time in her life, a group of believers crossed
Kim's path. They witnessed to her about the Christian faith and intro-
duced her to Jesus Christ. She gave her heart and life to him, and

became a member of his eternal family. She learned about forgiving others through God's Word. And she chose to forgive those who had so badly hurt her and left her forever scarred. Christ helped Kim make her decision. She did not forgive alone. Her natural reaction, like anybody else's, would be to hate American soldiers. She pardoned her offenders and released them from the debt of pain they had caused her. She forgave them because Christ had so graciously forgiven her.

Kim eventually met a young Vietnamese man who shared her newfound Christian faith. They fell in love, married, and set up a home where they could together serve Christ as their Lord. Kim became pregnant and gave birth to a son. Today, Kim, her husband, and their son live in Toronto. Kim and her husband hope to attend seminary in the future. They want to prepare themselves to become ministers of the gospel of Jesus Christ.

Kim is now thirty-three years old. She has never regretted her decision to forgive American soldiers. Recently, she traveled to Washington D.C., so she could visit the Vietnam War Memorial. She wanted to publicly extend her forgiveness to those who had bombed her family, burned her flesh, and killed her countrymen.

"I have suffered a lot from both physical and emotional pain," Kim said. "Sometimes I thought I could not live, but God saved my life and gave me faith and hope." Symbolizing her complete forgiveness, Kim knelt down and placed a wreath of flowers by the black polished granite Vietnam War memorial.

"Even if I could talk face to face with the pilot who dropped the bomb," Kim said, "I could tell him we cannot change history, but we should try to do good things for the present and for the future to promote peace."[1]

Scripture tells us that forgiveness should be accompanied by *kindness and compassion* (Rom. 12:20: "If your enemy is hungry, feed him; if he is thirsty, give him something to drink"); by *unlimited future forgiveness* (Matt. 18:22: "[Forgive] not seven times, but seventy-seven times," and Luke 17:3–4: "If your brother sins, rebuke him, and if he repents, forgive him. If he sins against you seven times in a day, and seven times comes back to you and says, 'I repent,' forgive him"); and by *love and prayer* (Matt. 5:44: "But I tell you: Love your enemies and pray for those who persecute you, that you may be sons of your Father in heaven").

After we forgive, Scripture encourages us to show kindness and compassion toward the forgiven person. We are to love and pray for the person. We are to seek God's good blessings on the person. It's the second part of forgiveness, the part that wishes the offender good things instead of bad.

As Grace Ketterman and David Hazard put it, "There is another part of forgiveness, a step that seems utterly impossible when we've been knocked flat on the ground: It's the step in which we seek the good of the offender."[2]

Daily Sunlight

☙ Interact with the Gardener

Tell God how you now feel after forgiving so many of your offenders. Describe the peace that forgiveness has brought into your heart and life.

Read Paul's words in Philippians 4:8: "Finally, brothers, whatever is true, whatever is noble, whatever is right, whatever is pure, whatever is lovely, whatever is admirable—if anything is excellent or praiseworthy—think about such things."

Name those things in your current life (after your journey of forgiveness) that are true, noble, right, pure, lovely, admirable, excellent, and praiseworthy.

Say a prayer to God and thank him for all the good things he has brought into your life.

James 1:17 tells us: "Every good and perfect gift is from above, coming down from the Father of the heavenly lights." Name the good and perfect gifts you have been given since you've traveled your journey toward forgiveness.

℮ Time to Grow

Michelle McKinney Hammond writes, "Praying for the one who hurt you is an important ingredient in the forgiveness process."[3]

You might be asking how you know if you have completely forgiven your offenders. Charles Stanley gives this answer: "When hurtful thoughts no longer linger/torture our minds; when we can know a certain peace; when we can think of the person and feel sorry/pity for him instead of anger/hatred; when we can pray for the person; for God to bless him."[4]

Using this principle, think about those offenders you have forgiven during the past weeks. Are you sure you have completely forgiven each one? Can you feel sorrow and pity for your offenders now instead of anger and hatred? Are you now able to take the next step in the forgiveness process? Are you ready to pray for each of your forgiven offenders? If so, pray for each one right now.

I am offering you two different prayers today. Depending on your answers to the previous questions, choose one of the following prayers to pray:

℮ Prayer

First Prayer:

Father, I cannot honestly say that I feel pity for [name your offenders]. I must admit I still feel anger and even hatred for them. I am not yet ready to pray for them. I am not yet ready to ask you to bless them. But, Father, I am open to your leading in these areas. I am trying, Father. I am struggling, and I desperately need your help. Please help me, Lord. I want my forgiveness for these offenders to be complete. I want to put their offenses to rest and become able to pray for them. In Jesus' name, amen.

Second Prayer:

Yes, Father! I can honestly say that I have completely forgiven all my offenders. Through this study, I have forgiven each one of them. I no longer feel resentment or bitterness in my heart toward any of them. I can honestly say, Lord, that I do feel sorry for them; I do pity them. And, Lord, I want to pray for each one today. I pray that you will forgive them, bring them to a saving knowledge of you if they are not believers, bring them close to you, and bless them in meaningful ways. Thank you, Father, for your precious gift of forgiveness. Thank you for the promised sweet peace that forgiveness has brought me. In Jesus' name, I pray, amen.

The POW
who decided to forgive

My bitter hatred . . . changed to loving pity.

Jacob DeShazer

Jacob "Jake" DeShazer had been on KP duty in a California Army camp on December 7 when he heard about Japan's sneak attack on Pearl Harbor. Shocked and angry, he wanted to retaliate personally. "Jap, just wait and see what we'll do to you!" he shouted in the Army kitchen.

The next month, DeShazer volunteered to fly with the Jimmy Doolittle Squadron in a secret mission to bomb Tokyo. As a gunner on one of the B–25 bombardiers on the carrier *Hornet*, Jake felt elated about getting revenge on the Japanese. The bombardiers brought havoc on Tokyo, destroying much of the city and killing many.

After the bombing raid, DeShazer and crew flew on toward China. But, on the journey, his plane ran out of fuel, and the men were forced to parachute into Japanese-held territory. Arrested as a POW, Jake spent the next forty months in confinement. Japanese guards kept them in a small dark prison cell—about six-by-six feet with one small window near the top. Three of his buddies were executed and another slowly died of starvation. The pain inflicted on him and the cruel treatment he endured almost drove him insane. He passionately hated the Japanese guards who so brutally tortured him.

After his first twenty-five months of imprisonment, the U.S. prisoners were given a Bible. Since Jake wasn't an officer, he had to let the others read it first. Then it was given to him for three weeks, and he read God's Word with fascination. He read the borrowed Bible until he understood God's message of salvation through his son, Jesus Christ. He asked the Lord to come into his heart and rule his life.

Jesus Christ changed Jake DeShazer in an unimaginable way. He began to see the cruel Japanese guards in a new light. The hatred he felt for them began to fade. He decided to forgive them for their inhumane treatment. Eventually, his hatred turned to love and concern.

"My bitter hatred . . . changed to loving pity," he remembers.

He asked God to forgive his torturers too. He resolved that should the United States win the war and he was freed from prison, he would someday return to Japan to introduce the Japanese to Jesus Christ.

In August 1945, paratroopers liberated DeShazer from his prison cell. After the war, Jake enrolled in Seattle Pacific College for some training. General MacArthur's staff asked DeShazer to write his POW experiences in a booklet, which was called "I Was a Prisoner of Japan." It told about the atrocities that had been committed against American war prisoners. It also told of DeShazer's forgiveness of those who had tortured him and included verses from the Bible.

Jake kept his word and returned to Japan as a missionary. He told the Japanese people his remarkable conversion story and gave them a copy of his booklet. He explained to them the power of forgiveness that God had shown him in his Word.

If Jake had decided not to forgive the Japanese torturers, would time have taken care of his resentment and bitterness? No, time usually causes more pain, not relief. Only forgiveness can heal pain, resentment, and bitterness. "Behind every act of forgiveness," writes Philip Yancey, "lies a wound of betrayal, and the pain of being betrayed does not easily fade away."[5] Even when we choose to forgive, our pain may linger for a long time. But forgiveness begins our journey toward the end of pain.

Today's story of God's forgiveness and Jake's forgiveness has been both beautiful and powerful. But it doesn't end here. Tomorrow we'll see what extraordinary events unfold.

Daily Sunlight

@ Interact with the Gardener

Ask God to give you the special grace to forgive those whose offenses against you, and against those you love, have been horribly inhumane. Ask the Lord to keep you from hating those people, like the Japanese guards, who abuse and torture you and your loved ones. Ask your loving heavenly Father to keep you and those you love from physical, emotional, and mental pain and cruelty inflicted by others.

@ Time to Grow

Drawing on the memory of your own forgiveness journey, what steps do you think Jake had to take before he could completely forgive the Japanese guards?

Imagine you could have a conversation with Jake. What would you want to ask him?

How did reading the Bible change DeShazer's attitude and life? How has reading and reflecting on Scripture during the past few weeks changed your attitude and life?

How did DeShazer begin to see the Japanese guards in a different light? How has Scripture and prayer helped you see your offenders in a different light over the past weeks?

In your own life, have you found that time does not heal pain, but instead causes deeper hatred, resentment, and bitterness? If so, describe the situation.

@ **Prayer**

Father, if Jacob DeShazer can forgive those inhumane guards who abused him, tortured him, and killed his friends, I can also forgive my future offenders. I can forgive the friend who betrays me, or lies to me, or slanders me; criminals who hurt me physically, emotionally, and mentally; as well as those offenders who hurt my loved ones. I realize forgiveness is the hardest thing I'll ever be called to do, Lord. But with your help, your guidance, and your strength, I will choose to forgive. In Jesus' name, amen.

The most unlikely convert

I came to the climactic drama — the Crucifixion. I read in Luke 23:34 the prayer of Jesus Christ at His death: "Father, forgive them; for they know not what they do." I was impressed that I was certainly one of those for whom He had prayed.

Mitsuo Fuchida

M itsuo Fuchida was the air-strike leader of the Japanese carrier force that attacked Pearl Harbor. Early on the morning of December 7, 1941, Commander Fuchida took off and led 360 planes toward Hawaii in the first surprise attack wave against the United States fleet. His goal? "To surprise and cripple the American naval force in the Pacific." Moments before the first bombs fell, he shouted the infamous radio message: "Tora! Tora! Tora!" meaning "Tiger! Tiger! Tiger!" This three-word message told Fuchida's superiors, Minoru Genda, and Admirals Nagumo and Yamamoto, that complete surprise had been achieved.

At 7:49 a.m, on that bright Sunday morning, the planes neared the Hawaiian Islands. From the air, Fuchida made a preliminary check of the harbor. He saw the entire American Pacific fleet peacefully at anchor in the inlet below. Then he smiled as he reached for the mike and ordered: "All squadrons, plunge in to attack!"

Fuchida remembers: "Like a hurricane out of nowhere, my torpedo planes, dive-bombers, and fighters struck suddenly with indescribable fury. As smoke began to billow and the proud battleships one by one started tilting, my heart was almost ablaze with joy."

Fuchida then directed the fifty level bombers to pelt not only Pearl Harbor, but the airfield, barracks, and dry docks nearby. He then circled overhead, assessed the damage, and reported the success of the attack to his superiors.

During that attack, Fuchida's bombers killed 3,077 U.S. Navy and 226 Army personnel and wounded 876 Navy and 396 Army personnel.

"It was the most thrilling exploit of my career," he said.

In early 1942, Fuchida also flew in air attacks in the Solomon Islands, Java, and the Indian Ocean. Just before the Battle of Midway (June 4, 1942) appendicitis left him unable to fly. He was reassigned to a staff job in Japan during the rest of the war.

Most Americans considered Fuchida an incredibly evil man who brought unexpected death and destruction to our armed forces. Japan honored Fuchida as a national hero.

After the war, with the Japanese forces disbanded, Fuchida returned to his home village near Osaka and began farming. He hated the boring work. He was later summoned by General Douglas MacArthur to testify at the war crime trials in Tokyo.

One day, as he stepped off the train in Tokyo's Shibuya Station, he saw an American handing out pamphlets. The American's name was Jacob DeShazer. He took the pamphlet "I Was a Prisoner of Japan" and put it in his pocket.

When Fuchida read about Jesus' crucifixion he was deeply touched by Jesus' words of forgiveness to those who had crucified him (see Luke 23:34). He understood within his soul that he, Fuchida, was one of the men Jesus had prayed for. He immediately sensed the love that Jesus wished to implant into his heart, even though he had slaughtered many men in the name of patriotism. Fuchida seemed to meet Jesus for the first time that moment. He understood the meaning of Christ's death as a substitute for his wickedness. He knelt in prayer, repented, and requested Christ to forgive his sins and change him from a bitter man into a Christian who lived for a higher purpose.

Fuchida gave his life to Christ and became a new creature. He came to love and obey the Savior whom he had always hated and ignored. His family and friends couldn't understand his decision, and they tried to persuade him to change his mind. But Fuchida held tight to his new faith in Christ. Jesus was truly the only one powerful enough to change this pilot's hardened heart.

But Fuchida's story is not over yet. He soon became a Christian evangelist. He teamed up with Jake DeShazer, and for the next thirty years, the two men traveled together throughout Japan and Asia telling others how Christ had transformed their lives from hate to love. As a result of their testimonies, tens of thousands of Japanese came to Christ.

Daily Sunlight

@ Interact with the Gardener

Reread Luke 23:34, the passage of Scripture that changed Mitsuo Fuchida's heart and life. What did this passage say to him personally? How did it bring him to Christ? What does this passage say to you personally?

@ Time to Grow

If you could sit down with Mitsuo Fuchida and have a private conversation, what questions would you want to ask him? Why?

If you have access to the internet, you can read Fuchida's own written testimony about his part in Pearl Harbor and his conversion experience. See "From Pearl Harbor to Calvary" at www.bli.org/pearlharbor/printmitsuo.htm.

@ Prayer

Father, what extraordinary circumstances you allow for people to read your Word and give their hearts to you! I learned with amazement the story of DeShazer and Fuchida—how they forgave each other and came to love each other, then joined together to bring the gospel to Japan. Amazing, Father! Thank you for the unique testimonies of these two men. I pray I can incorporate their love and forgiveness for others into my own everyday life. In Jesus' name, who brings the most unlikely people together, amen.

The ministry of forgiveness

I refuse to keep track of others' faults, because my Father has refused to keep track of mine.

Timothy Paul Jones

Jesus once told his disciple Peter this story: A servant owed a king a huge sum of money. The king wanted to settle the accounts with his servants, so he called them in. But one of his servants could not repay the king. He had no money. So the king ordered that the servant, his wife, his children, and his property be sold to repay the debt. But the servant fell to his knees and begged the king to be patient with him, to give him some time. He intended to pay back everything. The king felt sorry for the servant, so he canceled the debt. He wrote "paid in full" on his ledger and let him go.

The forgiven servant, however, went out and found a lesser servant who owed him a little money. He grabbed him, began to choke him, and demanded that he pay the small debt. The poor servant fell to his knees and begged for time and patience. He promised he would pay back the money he owed him.

But the forgiven servant refused. He threw the man in prison until he could pay the debt.

When the king heard what the forgiven servant had done, he ordered him to the palace. "You wicked servant," the king scolded him. "I canceled all that debt of yours because you begged me to. Shouldn't you have had mercy on your fellow servant just as I had on you?" In anger, the king threw the servant in jail to be tortured until he could pay back the huge amount of money he owed (see Matt. 18:21–35).

The story makes an essential point about forgiveness. Through Christ, God has forgiven us. He has adopted us into his family. We could never earn the huge amount of forgiveness God has bestowed on us. God's forgiveness cost him his son, Jesus. Therefore, we should reach out and forgive others who owe us much smaller debts.

God forgave Mitsuo Fuchida and Jacob DeShazer a huge debt, one that neither man could ever repay. He wrote "paid in full" on their accounts. In doing so, God expected the two men to also forgive the debts owed to them by sinful others. When they understood God's Word about forgiving others, their hate, thirst for revenge, resentment, and bitterness became forgiving love for their enemies. And their love and forgiveness became a full-time, soul-winning ministry to the Japanese people.

Only God can do that.

Daily Sunlight

℮ Interact with the Gardener

Read the parable of the unmerciful servant in Matthew 18:21–35. Envisioning the story, insert yourself into it. What part do you play? Why?

Reflect on these questions:

- What question did Peter ask to prompt Jesus' story?
- What is the primary point of Jesus' story?
- Does Jesus' story teach you any personal lessons about forgiving others?

@ Time to Grow

Timothy Paul Jones writes: "I refuse to keep track of others' faults, because my Father has refused to keep track of mine."[6]

- As you think about his statement in regards to your own life and situations, how does it apply to you?
- How can you apply this statement to your future journeys of forgiveness?

@ Prayer

Lord Jesus, thank you for your stories in Scripture that teach me more clearly the meaning of genuine and complete forgiveness. I have forgiven many people, Father, during the past six weeks. Please keep the weeds of bitterness from again growing in my heart. Help me to cultivate a forgiving heart. I know I will encounter future crises, tragedies, and pain. Please help me to name my offender, to name the offense, and to choose to forgive. Direct me to always take that first step of forgiveness. Follow me, Lord Jesus, into all the future journeys of forgiveness that I will, no doubt, be called to travel. In Jesus' name, I pray, amen.

Forgiving ourselves

> For, what other dungeon is so dark as one's own heart! What jailer so inexorable as one's self!
>
> Nathaniel Hawthorne

Today, we come to the last day of our devotional Bible study. Throughout this study, we have examined how God expects and enables us to forgive others who hurt, betray, wrong, and wound us. No matter how deep the pain, God gives us the capacity, the will, to forgive even those offenders who destroy our lives and the lives of those we love. We have learned that forgiveness has nothing to do with our feelings. Forgiveness is, instead, an act of our will. We will to forgive others because Jesus has so graciously forgiven us. We have explored and exposed, debunked and discarded the myths that keep Christian women from forgiving their offenders. We have shone the spotlight of Scripture into dark places where deceit hides.

We have accepted God's forgiveness. We have decided to forgive others. Now we come to our one final focus. We must forgive ourselves. And, surely, that's the hardest part in the process of forgiveness.

Allow me to introduce you to three famous men who had to seriously deal with forgiving themselves. No doubt, you have met them many times before.

Meet Peter—a fisherman-by-trade and an impetuous disciple of Jesus.

"I disowned Jesus at a time he needed me most. I cursed. I swore. 'I don't know the man!' I shouted to a servant girl in the courtyard where Jesus stood condemned. I had promised him long before the arrest 'even if I have to die with you, I will never disown you' (Mark 14:31). But I did. I denied him, and when he passed my way and looked into my eyes, I hated myself. I wanted to die. And every time a rooster crowed, I replayed the scene in my mind. Can I ever forgive myself?" (Matt. 26:69–75).

Meet Paul—an educated, well-connected, first-century Christian-killer.

"After the crucifixion, I tried to tear out the tiny root of Christ's seedling church. I bounty-hunted Christians. Chased them. Jailed them. Killed them. And in the middle of a long dark night, I can still see Stephen's face, as we stoned him and left him dying in a pool of blood. I've imprisoned my soul with self-condemnation" (Acts 6:8–8:1, especially 7:58 and 8:1).

Meet Judas—a dishonest disciple of Jesus and the group's treasurer.

"I betrayed Jesus for thirty pieces of silver—the price of a common slave. As I kissed him on the cheek, I handed him to the guards. I was the cause for his crucifixion. I feel as if I put the nails in his hands. And every time I hear a hammer hit a nail, I cringe. My crime condemns me. I will never forgive myself for this" (Matt. 26:14–16, 47–49).

Three guilty men. Three ghastly crimes. What became of these three men who imprisoned their souls with self-condemnation? Did they ever forgive themselves?

Peter did. Peter's strong faith became the rock on which Christ built his church (Matt. 16:18).

Paul did. Paul became a missionary-evangelist, planting Christ's seedling churches all over the known world.

But Judas didn't. He "was seized with remorse." He returned the coins, but he couldn't forgive himself. He "went away and hanged himself" (Matt. 27:3–5).

Surely, author Nathaniel Hawthorne describes Judas's heart when he writes: "For, what other dungeon is so dark as one's own heart! What jailer so inexorable as one's self!"[7]

You have chosen to forgive your offenders. I ask you now to choose to also forgive yourself. God has already forgiven you for all of your sins. "As far as the east is from the west, so far has he removed our transgressions from us" (Ps. 103:12).

The Father knows you, his daughter. He has compassion for you. He knows how you are formed—a fallible human being. He remembers that you are dust—capable of selfish sin (Ps. 103:13–14). If you are currently holding a grudge against yourself, it is time to forgive yourself and find the heart-peace your forgiveness will bring you. God does not want you to feel continual guilt. That's not the purpose of guilt. Good guilt comes to you like a wasp. It stings you, wakes you up to your sin and your need for forgiveness, and then it is gone. The sting on your flesh gradually heals.

Somehow, you and I must learn to distinguish "good" guilt from "bad" guilt—"true" guilt from "false" guilt. Dr. Paul Tournier writes: "'False guilt' is that which comes as a result of the judgments and suggestions of men. 'True guilt' is that which results from divine judgment."[8]

We can depend on true guilt to inform us of sin. "True guilt is like a built-in alarm system to notify us of the presence of a sin. Once we have confessed our sin, it is forgiven, and genuine guilt should cease."[9]

Allow good guilt to lead you to the process of healing, for it is, as Philip Yancey writes, "the spirit [that] speaks to us in the language of guilt so that we will take the steps necessary for healing ... The sense of guilt only serves its designed purpose if it presses us toward the God who promises forgiveness and restoration ... Guilt is only a symptom; we listen to it because it drives us toward the cure."[10]

Relinquish bad guilt from your heart, for it is a weed planted by Satan.

If you choose not to forgive yourself, you will become your own worst enemy, an "inexorable" jailer, a harsh condemning guard. Your punishment is self-directed. Until you decide to forgive yourself, to accept God's release from the bondage of your wrongdoing, you are locked in a dark deep dungeon of despair. And in that dungeon lies the recorded tape of your wrongdoing, a tape you play again and again in your mind. A tape that places guilt upon guilt on your heavy burdened heart.

Take your guilt to God. Punish yourself no longer. Stop trying to pay for your sin. Jesus has already done that. Ask God to take it away, to release you from its load. Then, lay it down, and walk away. Leave it lying on the trash pile where it belongs, the dump where God has placed your other forgiven sins. Thank God for your release and breathe in the fresh air of freedom. Flourish like a flower of his field. For our days to work in God's Kingdom are short (Ps. 103:15–16). We have no time to imprison ourselves when God wants to use us in his work.

Open your cell and be free. Accept peace and contentment. Produce fruit—future fruit for him. And if the enemy tries to replant the weeds of false guilt of a past forgiven sin, pull them up early and quickly. Do not allow them to grow in your heart. God does not want them rooted there. A heart filled with peace and contentment has no room for choking weeds.

Strive for complete forgiveness in your life. Remember what Charles Stanley said: "Forgiveness is never complete until, first, we have experienced the forgiveness of God, second, we can forgive others who have wronged us, and third, we are able to forgive ourselves."[11]

Daily Sunlight

@ Interact with the Gardener

Write the following statement on paper and stick it to your bathroom mirror. Read it each morning and each evening. Memorize it. "Forgiveness is never complete until, first, we have experienced the forgiveness of God, second, we can forgive others who have wronged us, and third, we are able to forgive ourselves."

Reread the following wise words by Dr. Paul Tournier regarding guilt. What do you learn from them?

> "Repentance means that recognition of guilt, and it is the sense of guilt which drives us to God and reveals to us the love and forgiveness of God."[12]

In your opinion, what is the role of "good guilt" and of "false guilt"? How can you recognize the difference between them when you feel guilt?

℮ Time to Grow

Describe the ways in which you can know that God has forgiven you of your sins.

Describe the ways in which you can know that you have forgiven those offenders who have sinned against you.

Are you willing to embark on another journey of forgiveness—the process of forgiving yourself? If so, write down every area in your life where you feel you need to forgive yourself. Over the next few weeks, daily review this list. Reread and review yesterday's study, and one by one apply the same principles of forgiveness to yourself that you have applied to your offenders.

Have you ever felt like this? "A primary reason we have no joy following our confession is that we do not really believe God has forgiven us. We think, 'How could God forgive me? What I have done is awful.' We remain under a load of guilt we refuse to lay down because of our unbelief."[13] Are you willing to begin the journey of forgiving yourself? If so, sign your name on the bottom of the sheet of paper, and write down the date.

℮ Prayer

Father, I can believe that you have forgiven me of my sins. I can also believe that I have truly forgiven all those who have hurt me. But, Lord, forgiving myself is another matter. How hard it is for me to forgive myself. Surely, my own heart is the "inexorable" harsh jailer. Teach me to forgive myself. Help me as I begin yet another journey of forgiveness—the journey to self-forgiveness. In Jesus' name, amen.

week
6

Weekly Watering

◊ A Light Sprinkling

Scripture tells us that forgiveness should be accompanied by *kindness and compassion* (Rom.12:20: "If your enemy is hungry, feed him; if he is thirsty, give him something to drink"); by *unlimited future forgiveness* (Matt. 18:22: "[Forgive] not seven times, but seventy-seven times," and Luke 17:3–4: "If your brother sins, rebuke him, and if he repents, forgive him. If he sins against you seven times in a day, and seven times comes back to you and says, 'I repent,' forgive him"); and by *love and prayer* (Matt. 5:44: "But I tell you: Love your enemies and pray for those who persecute you, that you may be sons of your Father in heaven").

1. Look up each Scripture passage cited above. Beside each one, write your own definition of the word, as it relates to forgiveness:

Kindness:

Compassion:

Unlimited future forgiveness:

Love:

Prayer:

2. Think of other words you might add to your list (i.e. generosity, mercy, grace, consideration, gentleness, thoughtfulness, sympathy, etc.).

◊ A Good Long Soaking

Let's quickly summarize the work you've done during the past six weeks:

1. You've met many other people within these pages who have been hurt and offended. Some have suffered life-threatening situations. Some have lost loved ones to murderers. Others have experienced lesser hurts—situations not life-threatening nor life-ending, but painful nonetheless. We have seen that however an offender chooses to hurt us, the hurt is real. Whether a murder or a criticism, whether a stranger's physical harm or a spouse's lie, whether a cruel physical beating or a friend's sharp words. Each offense needs our forgiveness.

2. You have recorded all those offenders you wanted to forgive. One by one, on index cards, you listed their names and hurtful acts. You made the decision to forgive your offenders, and you struggled in this journey for many weeks.

3. You recorded the reasons that kept you from forgiving your offenders. You examined ten different myths, and one by one worked through them all. You learned to separate forgiveness's truths from its myths.

4. Offender by offender, you asked God to help you forgive each one. You asked him to help you remember the lessons you learned, but not to dwell any longer on the offender or the offense.

5. You prayed for each offender by name and asked God to bless each offender in meaningful ways.

6. Then you looked inward at your own need to forgive yourself. Colleen Townsend Evans tells us what can happen when we refuse to forgive ourselves: "Our lives can become like overloaded cabooses—too heavy for our motors to pull. And unresolved guilt is the heaviest burden in the world. It slows us down, exhausts us, decreases our abilities to perform our tasks."[14]

7. You learned what it means to forgive yourself. And you began the new journey toward self-forgiveness.

Congratulations! You've finished the course, and you have done well.

Before I close, I want to leave you with a favorite quote. I pray it may help you as it has helped me in my own journey of forgiveness.

Robert Enright and Gayle Reed describe the outcome or "deepening phase" of forgiveness, the stage in which you yourself have entered: "In this [later] phase the forgiving individual begins to realize that he/she is gaining emotional relief from the process of forgiving ... the individual may discover a new purpose in life and an active concern for his/her community. Thus, the forgiver discovers the paradox of forgiveness: as we give to others the gifts of mercy, generosity, and moral love, we ourselves are healed."[15]

◊ Weekend Feeding

Father, thank you for the emotional relief I have gained from my six-week journey toward forgiving my offenders. With your help, I have pulled up the weeds of bitterness that took root within the soil of my heart. I have cultivated a forgiving heart—a heart ready to forgive my future offenders. I have truly discovered a new purpose in life and a more active concern for all people. I have also discovered the great paradox of forgiveness—how my own healing comes when I extend to others—especially those who hurt me—the rare gifts of mercy, generosity, moral love, and genuine forgiveness. Thank you, Father, for these treasures. In Jesus' name, I pray, amen.

Notes

Cultivating a forgiving heart

1. Chuck Lynch, *I Should Forgive, But...* (Nashville: Word, 1998), 57.

week 1: Forgiveness is a choice we make

1. Quoted in Grace Ketterman and David Hazard, *When You Can't Say "I Forgive You"* (Colorado Springs: NavPress, 2000), 77.
2. Ibid.
3. Ibid.
4. Colleen Townsend Evans, *Start Loving: The Miracle of Forgiving* (Garden City, NY: Doubleday, 1976), 63.
5. "Official End of Legendary Feud," CBS Broadcasting, Inc., 14 June 2003, http://www.cbsnews.com/stories/2003/06/13/earlyshow/saturday/main558660.shtml.
6. John Claypool, *Mending the Heart* (Boston: Cowley, 1999), 16.
7. Ketterman and Hazard, 29.
8. Alistair Begg, *The Hand of God* (Chicago: Moody, 1999), 161.
9. Sharon Cohen, "Homegrown Terrorist," *Associated Press,* 10 June 2001, http://cnews.canoe.ca/CNEWSFeatures0105/09_mcveigh-ap.html.
10. Rex W. Huppke, "Fellow Inmate Urges Mcveigh to Pursue Spiritual Redemption," *Associated Press,* 10 June 2001, http://www.reviewjournal.com/lvrj_home/2001/Jun-10-Sun-2001/news/16041945.html.
11. Charles W. Colson, "His Just Reward," *World,* 16 June 2001, http://www.worldmag.com/world/issue/06-16-01/closing_1.asp.
12. Lisa Beamer, *Let's Roll* (Wheaton, IL: Tyndale, 2002), 211.
13. Ibid., 213.
14. Ibid., 216.
15. Ibid., 213.

week 2: God chooses to forgive us

1. "Hate Crime Reports Up in Wake of Terrorist Attacks," CNN.com, 17 September 2001, http://www.cnn.com/2001/US/09/16/gen.hate.crimes.
2. Alan Cochrum, "Praying for Terrorists: A Scandalous Side to Mercy," *Ft. Worth Star-Telegram,* 2002, quoted in Amy Writing Awards, *The Amy Foundation* (Lansing, MI: 2002), 5.
3. Margaret Gramatky Alter, "The Unnatural Act of Forgiveness," *Christianity Today* (16 June 1997): 28.
4. Herschel Hobbs, *The Illustrated Life of Jesus* (Nashville: Holman, 2000), 155.
5. Michael Card, *Scribbling In the Sand* (Downers Grove, IL: InterVarsity, 2002), 15.

6. Ibid., 16.
7. Grace Ketterman and David Hazard, *When You Can't Say "I Forgive You"* (Colorado Springs: NavPress, 2000), 29.
8. C. H. Spurgeon, "The Quiet Heart," *Decision Magazine* (June 2002).

week 3: We must choose to forgive others

1. Helena Oliviero, "Freedom through Forgiveness," *The Atlanta Journal-Constitution* (2 November 2003): LS–LS3.
2. Ibid.
3. Paula Connor, *Walking in the Garden* (Englewood Cliffs, NJ: Prentice-Hall, 1984), 14.
4. John MacArthur, *In the Freedom and Power of Forgiveness,* quoted in Robert Jeffress, *When Forgiveness Doesn't Make Sense* (Colorado Springs: Waterbrook, 2000), 55.
5. You can read Simon Wiesenthal's story in *The Sunflower: On the Possibilities and Limits of Forgiveness.* The story and quotes are taken from L. Gregory Jones, reviewer, "Stumped by Repentance," *Christianity Today* (26 October 1998): 94.
6. Quoted in Lewis B. Smedes, *Forgive and Forget* (San Francisco: HarperSanFrancisco, 1984), 95.
7. Johann Christoph Arnold, *Seventy Times Seven: The Power of Forgiveness* (Farmington, PA: Plough, 1997), 8.
8. Quotes taken from Dawn Pick Benson, "The Healing Power of Forgiveness," *Homelife* (November 2000): 19. Information also came from Debbie Morris with Gregg Lewis, *Forgiving the Dead Man Walking* (Grand Rapids: Zondervan, 1998).
9. Oliviero, LS.

week 4: Exposing the myths

1. Bill Bartleman, "The state vs. Carneal," *The Paducah Sun,* 4 October 1998, http://www.skeptictank.org/hs/hatstrts.htm.
2. *USA Weekend,* "Education at the Millenium," 20–22 March 1998, http://www.usaweekend.com/98_issues/980322/980322bully_proof.html.
3. Missy Jenkins as told to Kay Lawing Gupton, "Finding Forgiveness," *Today's Christian Woman* (September–October 1998).
4. "Russell Yates Describes Wife As Victim," CNN.com, 19 March 2002, http://www.cnn.com/2002/LAW/03/18/yates.lkl.interview.
5. Ibid.
6. "Russell Yates Bids Farewell to His Five Children," CNN.com, 28 June 2001; and "Grief-Stricken Father Eulogizes Five Drowned Houston Children," *Associated Press,* 28 June 2001.
7. Lewis B. Smedes, "Keys to Forgiving," *Christianity Today,* 3 December 2001, http://www.christianitytoday.com/ct/2001/015/42.73.html.
8. Sharon Cohen, "Homegrown Terrorist," *Associated Press,* 10 June 2001, http://www.reviewjournal.com/lvrj_home/2001/Jun-10-Sun-2001/news/15991943.html.

9. Dan Barry with Maria Newman, "Boys Tell of Man's Beating, but None Use the Word 'Murder,'" *New York Times*, 29 June 2001, http://www.nytimes.com/2001/06/27/nyregion/27PATE.html.

10. Lewis B. Smedes, *The Art of Forgiving* (Nashville: Moorings, 1996), 182–83.

11. Ibid, 167.

12. Ibid.

13. Luigi Sandri and Edmund Doogue, "In Greece and Syria, Pope John Paul II Tries to Heal Ancient Wounds," *Christianity Today*, 9 May 2001, http://www.christianitytoday.com/ct/2001/119/34.0.html.

14. Ralph Tone, "Argentina First Messianic Synagogue Built," *Christianity Today*, 5 April 1999.

15. Frederick Buechner, *Telling Secrets* (San Francisco: HarperSanFrancisco: 1991), 32.

16. Smedes, *The Art of Forgiving,* 8.

17. Les Carter and Frank Minirth, *The Choosing to Forgive Workbook* (Nashville: Nelson, 1997), 56.

18. John Claypool, *Mending the Heart* (Cambridge, MA: Cowley, 1999), 5.

19. Smedes, "Keys to Forgiving."

20. Smedes, *The Art of Forgiving,* 167.

21. Robert Jeffress, *When Forgiveness Doesn't Make Sense* (Colorado Springs: Waterbrook, 2000), 88.

22. Buechner, 32.

week 5: Exposing more myths

1. Wendy Cole, "Forgiving a Murderer," *Time,* 5 April 1999, forgiveness.net.

2. Lewis B. Smedes, *The Art of Forgiving* (Nashville: Moorings, 1996), 59.

3. Frederick Buechner, *Telling Secrets* (San Francisco: HarperSanFrancisco, 1991), 33.

4. Desmond Tutu, *No Future Without Forgiveness* (NewYork: Doubleday, 1999), 272.

5. Tutu, 86.

6. Ibid., 156.

7. Ibid.,151.

8. John Cornyn, "Dennis Thurl Dowthitt Scheduled To Be Executed," *Media Advisory,* 6 March 2001, http://www.oag.state.tx.us/newspubs/newsarchive/2001/20010306dowthittfacts.htm.

9. Michael Graczyk, "In the Death Chamber, Eyes Betray Emotions," *Associated Press,* 10 June 2001.

10. Johann Christoph Arnold, *Seventy Times Seven* (Farmington, PA: Plough, 1997), 67–69.

11. "Deadly Submission?" *Discipleship Journal* (July–August 2001): 14.

12. Ibid.

13. Frank A. Thomas, *They Like to Never Quit Praisin' God* (Cleveland: Pilgrim, 1997), 59–60.

14. Karl Menninger, *Whatever Became of Sin?* (New York: Hawthorn, 1973), 168.

15. Smedes, 159.
16. Paul Meier, *Don't Let Jerks Get the Best of You* (Nashville: Nelson, 1993), 185.
17. Quoted in Annette LaPlaca, "Clearing the Air," *Marriage Partnership* (Fall 1996).
18. Meier, 185.
19. Robert Jeffress, *When Forgiveness Doesn't Make Sense* (Colorado Springs: Waterbrook, 2000), 43.
20. Brandon Biggs interviewed by Larry King, *Larry King Live,* CNN, 7 July 2003.
21. Debbie Morris, *Forgiving the Dead Man Walking* (Grand Rapids: Zondervan, 1998), 246.
22. Ibid.
23. Smedes, 27.
24. William A. Meninger, *The Process of Forgiveness* (New York: Continuum, 1996), 30.
25. Tutu, 271.

week 6: Forgiving others frees us to flourish

1. Quoted in Charles Colson and Nancy Pearcey, "Victory Over Napalm," *Christianity Today* (3 March 1997).
2. Grace Ketterman and David Hazard, *When You Can't Say "I Forgive You"* (Colorado Springs: Navpress, 2000), 171.
3. Michelle McKinney Hammond, *What Becomes of the Brokenhearted* (Eugene, OR: Harvest House, 2001), 138.
4. Charles Stanley, *Forgiveness* (Nashville: Oliver-Nelson , 1987), 132.
5. Philip Yancey, *What's So Amazing about Grace?* (Grand Rapids: Zondervan, 1997), 85.
6. Timothy Paul Jones, *Prayers Jesus Prayed* (Ann Arbor, MI: Servant, 2002), 44.
7. Nathaniel Hawthorne, *The House of the Seven Gables* (New York: Penguin, 1990), 151.
8. Paul Tournier, *Guilt and Grace* (New York: Harper and Row, 1962), 67.
9. Chuck Lynch, *I Should Forgive, But . . .* (Nashville: Word, 1998), 128.
10. Philip Yancey, "Guilt Good and Bad," *Christianity Today* (18 November 2002): 112.
11. Stanley, 137.
12. Tournier, 173.
13. Stanley, 103.
14. Colleen Townsend Evans, *Start Loving: The Miracle of Forgiving* (Garden City, NY: Doubleday, 1976), 44.
15. Robert Enright and Gayle Reed, "A Process Model of Forgiving," International Forgiveness Institute, 27 June 2001, http://www.forgivenessinstitute.org/IFI/Whatis/process_model.htm.